THE MAD TRAPPER

The MAD TRAPPER

UNEARTHING A MYSTERY

Barbara Smith

VICTORIA • VANCOUVER • CALGARY

Heritage House Publishing Company Ltd.
#108 – 17665 66A Avenue
Surrey, BC V3S 2A7
www.heritagehouse.ca

Heritage House Publishing Company Ltd.
PO Box 468
Custer, WA 98240-0468

Library and Archives Canada Cataloguing in Publication

Smith, Barbara, 1947–
    The mad trapper: unearthing a mystery / Barbara Smith.

ISBN 978-1-894974-53-0

    1. Johnson, Albert, d. 1932. 2. Police murders—Rat River Region (Yukon and N.W.T.). 3. Trappers—Northwest Territories—Biography. 4. Criminals—Northwest Territories—Biography. 5. Exhumation—Northwest Territories—Aklavik. I. Title.

FC4172.1.J64S65 2009   971.9'202092   C2009-900271-X

Library of Congress Control Number: 2009920201

Cover and book design by Frances Hunter
Cover photo of Lynne Bell and David Sweet examining the skeleton
    of the Mad Trapper by Matthew Spidell
Historical documents courtesy of RCMP Museum
Facial-reconstruction image on page 137 reproduced courtesy
    of Andrea Stevenson Won, Biomodal

Printed in Canada

Heritage House acknowledges the financial support for its publishing program from the Government of Canada through the Book Publishing Industry Development Program (BPIDP), Canada Council for the Arts and the province of British Columbia through the British Columbia Arts Council and the Book Publishing Tax Credit.

For Bob
With love and gratitude

CONTENTS

Introduction   9

PART ONE

The Legendary Chase   14

Mystery Man   40

PART TWO

A New Approach to Solving
an Old Mystery   54

The Exhumation Begins   63

The Mad Trapper Resurfaces   74

PART THREE

Forensics in the Field   90

Building a Profile   111

Looking for a Match   138

Conclusion   149

Endnotes   153

Select Bibliography   155

John Evans of the Canadian Police Research Centre (bottom left), forensic anthropologist Owen Beattie and odontologist David Sweet pore over the skull of the Mad Trapper.
PHOTO BY MATTHEW SPIDELL

Introduction

DECADES AGO, WHEN I FIRST heard the tale of how the Mad Trapper of Rat River had led Northwest Territories RCMP officers on a seven-week midwinter manhunt in the early 1930s, I was fascinated, but I presumed that the saga of the man calling himself Albert Johnson was a piece of fiction. No one could deny it was a great story, but I did not believe it was factual: the entire premise was too outlandish to be believed. A man could not survive outdoors during an Arctic winter for as long as Johnson had on wits and determination alone—and certainly not while evading a well-organized, well-equipped posse of pursuers. More outlandish still was the proposition that this pursuit had gone on for almost two months and that in the end, the RCMP had caught a mystery man. The concept was preposterous and seemed more like the plot of a 1950s comic book than an actual historical event. It had to be a legend, a piece of fiction that perhaps, at best, was based on actual events.

Still, as an author of books about local folklore and social history, I could not resist looking into the matter as thoroughly as I could. What I found was that not only was the story fascinating, it was also most assuredly factual. For the next 20 or more years, whenever another book about the Mad Trapper came out, or another article ran in a magazine or newspaper, I made sure to read it to see what was being offered as new information.

However, as intriguing as the topic of the Mad Trapper was, pursuing it for a book of my own seemed pointless, because I felt his amazing feats and the enticing mystery of his unknown identity had already been amply covered. And so I set aside the idea and went about finding other interesting subjects to write about.

Although writing is a solitary occupation, generating topics for writing projects can be a very social undertaking. For this reason, I consider myself tremendously fortunate to have scriptwriters, filmmakers and other authors as friends. An hour's conversation at a café with any one of these people can generate concepts that lead to workable enterprises. Toward that end, my long-time friend and Emmy Award-winning producer Michael Jorgensen and I make a point of getting together whenever our schedules allow it.

One such informal meeting took place in 2003. Michael's production company, Myth Merchant Films, had been developing a television documentary about the Mad Trapper based on discussions with someone who had anecdotal evidence suggesting that he shared a genetic link with the legendary fugitive. This man's story was intriguing, and interested Michael and his business partner, Carrie Gour. Although their initial approach to the project fell through completely, the filmmakers' interest in the Mad Trapper endured. Consequently, Carrie and Michael formed plans for a considerably more ambitious project, committing themselves to doing everything within their power to obtain permission to exhume Albert Johnson's body in the hamlet of Aklavik, in Canada's Northwest Territories. The idea was to have forensic scientists thoroughly investigate his remains, harvest samples for DNA comparison with potential kin and make a documentary about their findings. They presumed—correctly, as it turned out—that media coverage of the exhumation would draw candidates to Myth Merchant's website.

What an honour it was to be asked by Michael to join the Myth Merchant team for this history-making project. My role, he explained, in addition to some administrative duties, would be to follow the filmmakers through their ambitious and complex undertaking, recording information as it was uncovered and producing a companion book to their television documentary. My long fascination with the mysterious Albert Johnson quickly became a near-obsession because Myth Merchant's project could have a most rewarding conclusion: finding out exactly, once and for all, who the man known as the Mad Trapper of Rat River really was.

When he first appeared in Fort McPherson, Northwest Territories, and gave his name as Albert Johnson, no one had any reason to wonder whether that was his real name or an alias. It was his behaviour, his apparent strong desire not to socialize or share any information about himself, that made people wonder about him. Who was he really? Why was he in the Arctic? Where had he come from?

Our journey of discovery was about to begin.

The Mad Trapper's frozen post-mortem
smile is an image that is hard to forget.

PART **ONE**

The Legendary **Chase**

Saturday, December 26, 1931

A few hours before daybreak on Boxing Day, 1931, Royal Canadian Mounted Police (RCMP) Constable Alfred King and Special Constable Joe Bernard harnessed a team of sled dogs and mushed west from their Arctic Red River detachment in the Northwest Territories, at the confluence of the Mackenzie and Arctic Red rivers. They were heading out to investigate an accusation made by Aboriginal trappers who lived and worked along the Rat River that someone had been interfering with their traplines.

The man in charge of the Arctic Red River detachment, Constable Edgar Millen, knew that the only newcomer to the area of late was a taciturn trapper known as Albert Johnson, who had arrived the previous summer. In July 1931, Millen had spoken to this man in a store at Fort McPherson. He had noticed that the newcomer seemed to be carrying a large amount of money and also that he seemed very quiet—but not so much as to cause concern, especially in a time and place where eccentricities were common. He also noticed that the stranger spoke with a trace of a Scandinavian accent.

Constable Millen introduced himself to Johnson. Police protocol in this remote area was to make sure everyone within the jurisdiction was mentally and physically prepared for the arduous conditions of the extreme north. The constable's exchange with the stranger was cursory, and had it been his only interaction with Johnson, the young officer might never have given the man's existence another thought. About a month later, however, Millen's commanding officer, Inspector Alexander Eames, sent him a stern written rebuke, taking him to task for not having questioned the man calling himself Albert Johnson as thoroughly as he should have.

Furthermore, since the initial encounter in July, the newcomer had shown himself to be not just an uncommunicative and unfriendly person, but also an uncooperative one who had not purchased a trapping licence. This factor further fuelled suspicions that he might be the one guilty of interfering with his Aboriginal neighbours' traplines—a serious accusation, as families' livelihoods depended almost exclusively on the sale of pelts.

However, one officer's later research revealed that the Aboriginal trappers' accusations might not have been truthful. RCMP Constable William Carter investigated the original complaint in the spring of 1932 and "found an entirely different story. Evidently, Johnson had roughly told them to take off and had even pointed a gun at them, when they came a-visiting at Johnson's cabin."

Carter's report goes on to say:

> Knowing Indians very well, I can imagine they were curious about Johnson and wanted to know what he was doing in their trap area. Also, it is customary to give an Indian a drink of tea and something to eat. With repeated visits, Johnson's food supply would soon be depleted, so he was stopping the visits in the bud.
>
> Retaliating, the Indians had decided to complain about Johnson to drive him out of the country, and this was what started the long series of "hunts" which terminated in his death.[1]

In any case, it appeared that the Aboriginal neighbours in question had reason to lodge a complaint with the RCMP about Albert Johnson. Even though they did not know the name of the man who had pointed the gun at them, Constable Millen strongly suspected from their description that it was the same person he had interviewed the previous summer: the man who had given his name as Albert Johnson.

Despite the severe winter travelling conditions and knowing little about the offender, Constable King and Special Constable Bernard did not anticipate that the assignment would be extraordinary in any way. They would simply make their way by dog team to Johnson's cabin, order him to leave other people's lines alone and remind him to apply for his own trapping licence. Both constables were experienced with travel during the Arctic winter, and were confident that they could complete the 220-kilometre round trip in time to join their friends and colleagues at a New Year's Eve party.

At that latitude (68 degrees north), only a few days after the longest night of the year, twilight lingers for a few hours around noon before giving way again to the dark of night. With temperatures hovering between -30°c and -50°c, the two police officers were grateful to spend their first night in the small community of Fort McPherson, approximately 70 kilometres west of their detachment. The next night, December 27, they were not so fortunate; they had to camp out in the snow and frigid cold near the mouth of the Rat River, their only consolation being that they did not have much farther left to travel.

Monday, December 28, 1931

King and Bernard arrived at the newcomer's homestead around mid-morning and were heartened to see smoke billowing from the chimney of the spartan log cabin and the occupant's handmade willow-frame caribou-hide snowshoes propped up against an exterior wall. Albert Johnson was obviously at home, so the officers had every reason to believe their dealings with him would be wrapped up quickly.

King knocked on the door with his heavily mittened hand. Much to his surprise, there was no answer. He called out to Johnson, identifying himself as a police officer. Still there was no answer. He called out again, adding that he only wanted to speak to him. Still there was no response. After waiting an hour in the bitter cold, the two constables left, knowing it was pointless to remain any longer. They also knew that this was no longer a routine investigation. Johnson had broken a long-held code of the North by not opening his door to someone who had asked to be let in. Any thoughts that Bernard and King had been entertaining about attending a New Year's Eve celebration were blown away as effectively as if by the howling Arctic wind. Instead, they needed to go to Aklavik, roughly 80 kilometres away, where they would ask their commanding officer, Inspector Eames, to issue a search warrant.

Wednesday, December 30, 1931

Inspector Eames immediately agreed that the situation with Johnson needed to be taken very seriously. He not only issued the warrant as requested, but had Special Constable Lazarus Sittichinli, Constable Robert McDowell and an additional team of dogs accompany King and Bernard on their return visit.

Thursday, December 31, 1931

By the last day of the year, the cold had intensified and the wind had picked up, creating a temperature that was the equivalent of -67°C. These were obviously extremely dangerous conditions. If hell were cold, surely it would have borne a close resemblance to these bleak and almost unbearable circumstances.

After a 28-hour trip, the four-man posse arrived at Johnson's cabin. It was just after 10:30 a.m. The Arctic dawn was breaking and, as on the previous visit, there was every indication that Johnson was in his cabin. Constable King knocked on the door and called out, identifying himself as a police officer and asking Johnson to open the door. This time the officer's presence was acknowledged immediately—with the crack of gunfire. King crumpled to the snow, the bullet lodged in his chest. McDowell opened fire. Even if he could not manage a clear shot at Johnson, he could at least divert the man's attention from King, who had obviously been seriously wounded. A vicious gunfight ensued, creating the necessary but potentially deadly diversion. While bullets whizzed everywhere around McDowell, King dragged himself, agonizingly slowly, out of the line of fire.

The three uninjured Mounties strapped their colleague to a sled. King was bleeding profusely, and his companions knew he would soon die if they did not get proper medical attention for him as soon as possible. Pushing the dog teams as fast as they dared, the men raced the 129 kilometres to the Aklavik hospital in a record-breaking 20 hours. One of the dogs collapsed and died from exhaustion along the route, but the men's efforts paid off: King was still alive.

And now Albert Johnson was wanted on a much more serious charge—that of the attempted murder of an RCMP officer.

Friday, January 1, 1932

Inspector Eames knew he had to plan his reaction to this worrisome situation carefully. Johnson was evidently not only dangerous, but also unpredictable, and therefore a very real threat. The only reasonable way to contain that danger was to send enough men, dogs and supplies to keep Johnson's cabin surrounded. But Inspector Eames' resources were limited, and he certainly could not leave the rest of the area without police protection. The inspector decided he would have to bolster his meagre force with civilians, special constables and men from the Royal Canadian Signal Corps Army base in Aklavik, a move that led to news about the attempt on Constable King's life spreading quickly to the outside world. This in turn meant the RCMP's international reputation was under public scrutiny and very much at stake, increasing the importance of a timely arrest. Inspector Eames still needed several days to organize the men, dogs, provisions and weapons—which in this case even included dynamite.

Monday, January 4, 1932

By morning, the inspector, seven carefully selected men and two dog teams set out from the RCMP post, destined for the bunker-like shack 32 kilometres from the mouth of the Rat River. News-hungry reporters had already dubbed the cabin's dangerous occupant the "Mad Trapper," the moniker being a reference to Johnson's supposed interference with

MEMBERS OF THE FINAL GROUND POSSE

- RCMP Inspector Alexander Eames
- RCMP Constable Sid May (no relation to Wop May)
- RCMP Constable William Carter
- Special Constable Joe Verville
- Special Constable Karl Garlund
- Special Constable John Moses
- Royal Canadian Signal Corps Quartermaster Earl "Heps" Hersey
- Royal Canadian Signal Corps Quartermaster Sergeant R.F. Riddell
- Volunteers Frank Jackson and former RCMP constable Constant Ethier

```
PLEASE          INSTRUCT        IF
  214             214            214
 16740           12024          11138
 16954           12241          11352
PORTABILITY     INVADER        IMPORTUNATENESS


PERMISSIBLE     TO           BURY        JOHNSON
  214           214           214
 16338         22484         03250
 16552         22698         03464
PICNIC         TROTTING      CANNON      JOHNSON


WITHOUT        BURIAL        SERVICE      OR
  214           214           214         214
 23829         03227         20447       15570
 24043         03441         20661       15784
DONALD         CANDENT       SHOW        OWED
            PUBLIC 214
              17799
              18013   QUADRILATERAL

DISCLOSURE
DISCLOSING Trotting LOCATION   OF        GRAVE
  214           214           214         214
 07004         13470         15439       10218
 07218         13684         15653       10432
DISSATISFIED   LUXURIATING   OSPREY      HAIR.
```

Strangely, the RCMP felt confidentiality was important during the 1932 manhunt. This is a code sheet that it used to keep its communications secret.

the Natives' traplines and the suspicion that he'd gone insane from isolation. That label was sensational enough to attract the purple journalists of the era.[2]

Saturday, January 9, 1932

Late in the morning, after a gruelling journey through swirling snow-storms, Inspector Eames and his seven men arrived, cold and tired, at Johnson's cabin. The commanding officer ordered his men to surround the promontory where the cabin stood while remaining out of sight as he yelled a warning to Johnson.

"Give yourself up! We have you surrounded," Eames shouted before adding words he hoped would ease Johnson's sense of desperation and therefore make the situation a little safer for the police. "The man you shot isn't dead. You're not wanted for murder."

Utter silence was the only reply. They had no way of knowing Johnson's silence was an eerie precursor of what was to come. Throughout the entire ordeal, the outlaw calling himself Albert Johnson was never heard to speak a word.

After commanding Johnson a third time to give himself up, Inspector Eames ordered his men to move toward the cabin. The fugitive was obviously watching from inside, because as soon as the policemen came within range, he began firing round after round in their direction, through ports in the cabin walls. The wanted man may have been badly outnumbered, but he had two important advantages—a clear sightline and shelter from the frigid weather—while the lawmen were forced to lie still, unprotected, in -30°c temperatures, with the Arctic wind relentlessly sucking heat from their bodies.

Inspector Eames could soon see that firepower alone was not going to roust this determined criminal from his hiding place. He ordered his men to warm the dynamite, using the only method available—tucking the frozen explosives inside their clothes, in hopes that the charges would thaw from the men's body heat. When the explosives were deemed ready for use, each member of the party took turns bravely running through the waist-high snow toward the cabin and lobbing a makeshift bomb where he hoped it would do the most destruction to the shack. After hours of effort, the dynamite supply had dwindled but the extreme cold had made the charges all but ineffective, and there had been little damage done to the cabin. The men were exhausted. Worse, supplies for themselves and their dogs were getting critically low.

Sunday, January 10, 1932

By 3:00 a.m., in a last-ditch attempt to literally blow Johnson's cover, Knut Lang, the tallest and lankiest of the men Eames had brought with him, lit the fuse on a bundle of dynamite. Lang ran toward the cabin and, at a point he deemed both safe for him and dangerous for the occupant, threw the bomb with all his considerable might and skill.

LITTLE-KNOWN FACTS ABOUT THE CASE OF THE MAD TRAPPER

- John Moses, one of the special constables involved in the 1932 manhunt and the final shootout that followed it, threw away his gun after the shootout because he didn't want to hunt food for his family with a gun that had killed a human being.
- Hospitalization in Aklavik for Sergeant Hersey and Constable King while they recovered from the injuries inflicted by the Mad Trapper's bullets cost 50 cents per day.
- Volunteer posse members received between $5 and $7 for each day they were involved in the hunt. A.E. Acland, superintendent of the RCMP's G division, deemed $10 per day to be "excessive."
- Canadian Airways Limited was paid $4,391.65 for the services of Wop May, his mechanic Jack Bowen and the use of the plane during the final weeks of the hunt.
- The Herculean hunt for the Mad Trapper popularized the saying "the Mounties always get their man."

The sizzling bundle landed squarely on the shack's roof and seconds later a tremendous blast blew the building to bits.[3]

Although Eames and his posse would have preferred to take Albert Johnson alive, by now they simply hoped the silence hanging over the ruined cabin meant they would find a recognizable body. The exhausting nine-hour siege was over at last—or so they thought.

As the smoke cleared, the men approached the wrecked cabin. One of the searchers carried a flashlight to help guide the way. Seconds later, according to the most commonly told account of the events that followed, a bullet knocked the light from the man's hand.

Special constables Karl Garlund and Knut Lang later filed a report to their superiors indicating that "the door of Johnson's cabin had been jarred open, but it was dark inside and nothing could be seen of Johnson when several men had rushed by, peering in at the same time. So it was finally decided to tie a flashlight on a stick. A man would then shine it in the doorway while hiding around to one side, while another rushed by the opening to see inside. The action was carried out but as one rushed by the door the flashlight was shot out—but not out of a hand."

By now, it was quite clear that Albert Johnson was not dead; he was not even ready to give up his fight. The police officers knew they were dealing with a cunning and apparently fearless adversary. The exhausted men huddled together to plan their next move. An hour later, recognizing that their resources were completely spent, they began the cold, difficult trek back to Aklavik.

Thursday, January 14, 1932

Inspector Eames radioed a message to Constable Millen at the Arctic Red River detachment, instructing him and Karl Garlund, an experienced civilian tracker who had been part of Eames' posse as a special constable on January 9, to check on the ruins of Johnson's cabin and report on what they found.

Saturday, January 16, 1932

Millen and Garlund found the ruins of the cabin deserted. It was apparent that Albert Johnson had fled. Clearly, he would rather risk freezing to death in an attempt to escape than be brought in alive by the police. A desperate Arctic manhunt had begun, and it had not begun well. Heavy snow had fallen, and any tracks Johnson would have left with his distinctive snowshoes were now buried.

From Aklavik, Inspector Eames ordered the men to stay and watch over the cabin site in case Johnson came back. That same day, a fresh posse of seven more men driving dog teams set out for the cabin on Eames' orders. These new recruits included two officers from Aklavik's Army Signal Corps detachment who were armed with a two-way radio and a stash of homemade bombs. The weather had not improved; the group had to make its way through the same vicious snowstorm that had buried Johnson's snowshoe tracks. Even with dog teams, the searchers' progress was painfully slow. The low temperatures and mere hours-long twilight, followed by dark, extremely cold nights, were constant threats to everyone's safety.

Monday, January 18, 1932

After fighting the unrelenting blizzard for two days, the men finally made it to the mouth of the Rat River, 14.5 kilometres from Albert Johnson's cabin. Here, a messenger from Millen's group of searchers gave them the disheartening news that the fugitive was still on the run. After setting up a base camp, they spent the next four days fruitlessly combing the frozen countryside. Any tracks that might have led them to the fugitive had been blown away by the howling wind and whirling snow.

Friday, January 22, 1932

Inspector Eames knew the supplies for this huge search party would run out quickly. He made the difficult decision to dismiss a dozen volunteer searchers in order to ensure that the core group could remain on the job for another week, if necessary.

Monday, January 25, 1932

The wind finally let up enough that on one of their ongoing daily searches, the men spotted tracks left by Johnson's distinctive snowshoes. It appeared he was heading west to the Richardson Mountains.

Thursday, January 28, 1932

The men were heartened by the arrival of a Native tracking guide, but frustrated at his news that two shots had been heard further west, near the Bear River. It was a safe presumption that the gunfire had been Johnson hunting for food. He seemed to be tantalizingly near, yet still elusive.

Friday, January 29, 1932

The searchers were tired, discouraged and baffled. If *they* were exhausted, it was difficult to imagine how their quarry was able to keep going. Temperatures hovered at a potentially fatal -50°c.

Although they were no closer to catching Albert Johnson, they were at least becoming familiar with his methods. The desperate man seemed to avoid leaving tracks, by walking either on ice blown bare of snow or over ground trampled by caribou herds. When he did leave tracks, it was as if he had done so on purpose, to toy with his would-be captors. Having been led in the entirely opposite direction, the searchers realized that he sometimes put his snowshoes on backwards. Other times, his tracks indicated that he had walked in an exaggerated zigzag pattern. Even though this meant he would have had to walk twice the distance, doing so provided an occasional vantage point from which he could spot the men coming after him.

Johnson did not have the luxury of a dog team, so he was carrying all his supplies on his back—yet the well-equipped lawmen could not catch him. Did Johnson have some sort of superhuman power? Was he more experienced with northern travel than the police were? Could it be that he was also experienced at eluding the law? As always, the questions all boiled down to "Who *is* this man?"

Later in the day, while trying to find a location from which to spot Johnson, some of the searchers climbed a ridge above a creek. They sighted something that looked as though it could be one of Johnson's temporary camps, but the fugitive was not there.

Saturday, January 30, 1932

By late morning, the searchers had divided into teams in order to cover as much territory as possible. Constable Millen's group had not gone far when they heard a man coughing. Slowly and silently they moved toward the sound and spotted the now-familiar pattern left by the fugitive's snowshoes. His tracks led into a stand of trees. Soon they were roughly 15 metres from Albert Johnson, who clearly had not detected their presence.

Because of the bitter cold, waiting him out was potentially lethal. They could not lie still; it was time to strike.

As they moved in on him, one of the men in the posse slipped on the steep bank, drawing Johnson's attention. The outlaw angled himself toward the sudden noise, aimed his rifle and began shooting. The lawmen returned his fire. After a particularly fast volley of bullets into Johnson's hiding place, there was nothing but silence. The constables waited, still and quiet. After two hours in an unmercifully frigid silence, as the perpetually grey daytime sky began to darken toward nightfall, Millen signalled his men to move in on their prey. Seconds later, shots rang out from Johnson's hiding place. Most of the searchers scrambled for cover, but Millen held his ground, aimed and shot twice. Johnson returned each shot—plus one more.

It was the third bullet from the fugitive's gun that struck Millen in the chest. Special Constable Garlund, a well-respected member of the manhunt team, slithered toward his comrade's prone body. He reached out and untied the badly injured constable's bootlaces, then retied them to form a makeshift handle. Using the laces, he pulled Millen toward him, but it was too late. RCMP Constable Edgar Millen was dead at the age of 31.

The remaining men on Millen's team assaulted the thicket with round after round of gunfire, but there was no sign of the fugitive.

Angry and frustrated, two of the searchers built an elevated platform to keep Millen's body away from scavenging animals, while a third rushed off with a dog team to let the other searchers and police headquarters in Aklavik know about the tragedy.

Tuesday, February 2, 1932

Inspector Eames acted immediately, putting out a call for volunteer searchers. He also contacted the federal government with a previously unheard-of request: he wanted an aircraft with an experienced pilot to join the hunt. Even though a plane had never been used in Canadian crime fighting before, the hunt for the Mad Trapper was deemed significant enough to set this precedent. First World War flying ace Wilfrid "Wop" May and his long-time mechanic, Jack Bowen, were immediately dispatched in a Bellanca Pacemaker monoplane.

Wednesday, February 3, 1932

The weather worsened. A blizzard raged, creating blinding conditions that meant even a pilot of May's calibre could fly only short distances at a time. The ground searchers were not faring any better. Blowing snow covered Johnson's tracks as soon as he made them. All they could do was keep looking for him with the presumption that he might be heading west toward Alaska.

Friday, February 5, 1932

When the searchers did find tracks that day, it was evident that Johnson had made them for the sole purpose of frustrating and confusing his pursuers. In one spot, two sets of tracks ran parallel, while in another place, two sets of tracks seemed to lead in opposite directions. The posse again divided, this time into two groups, each following one set of tracks. Hours later, the exhausted men found themselves facing one another. Johnson had tricked them once more. The killer's endurance

Pilot Wilfrid "Wop" May (left) and flight mechanic Jack Bowen stand beside their Bellanca Pacemaker monoplane. Their skill and diligence, and the far-ranging views from the aircraft, were pivotal in ending the gruelling Arctic manhunt. GLENBOW ARCHIVES NA-1258-106

and cunning were terrifying. Even more alarming was the fact that by now he'd had plenty of opportunity to be well clear of the RCMP's jurisdiction, yet he had lingered. Was he taking a perverse delight in the apparent torment of his pursuers?

Journalists had dubbed him the "Mad Trapper," but his trackers were using different and considerably more accurate descriptors, such as "shrewd," "resolute," "capable," "tough" and "desperate."

Sunday, February 7, 1932

After bucking heavy winter storms on their flight path from Edmonton, Alberta, to the Mackenzie Delta, Wop May and Jack Bowen, together with an additional RCMP constable, William Carter (who wrote his own comprehensive report about the chase in 1932), arrived to help with the hunt. The pilot and his mechanic were a veteran team with lots of northern experience. Not only was this aircrew able to search the difficult terrain from the sky, but it could also deliver food and equipment to the posses in a fraction of the time the dogsled teams had taken to perform the task.

Monday, February 8, 1932

May and Bowen flew provisions from Aklavik to the searchers' base camp, and on their return flight they carried out Millen's body. Just hours later, however, the weather became too dangerous for flight. May's plane was grounded, and within a few hours it was completely buried in snow.

Tuesday, February 9, 1932

As soon as the wind and snow had calmed, May and Bowen began to dig, but it took hours to free the single-engine plane from its covering of deep snow. Once they were finally airborne, they dropped additional supplies to the searchers.

Friday, February 12, 1932

The severe weather had cost the searchers days of valuable time. They were positive, though, that their quarry could not be far away. A formidable geographic barrier, the Richardson Mountains—the most northerly tip of the Rockies—lay ahead. They were certain that no one could make it over those mountains in such horrendous conditions.

THE MAD TRAPPER'S CAMP

RCMP Constable William Carter, who was "detailed to take Constable Millen's body to the plane . . . by dog team . . . a distance of about 15 miles," examined the fugitive's makeshift camp at the site where Constable Millen was killed. Constable Carter recalled finding that a "piece of crusty snow had been placed near the fire on a twig, evidently so that it would melt into a cup (a tin cup . . . was found later in his packsack). All of his utensils had been damaged by rifle fire . . . the imprint of the tin cup was in the snow . . . " Carter deduced that Johnson had been melting snow to make tea.[4]

Their confidence was dashed that afternoon, however, when a local hunter reported having seen the Trapper's tracks heading over a mountain pass.

Sunday, February 14, 1932

The ground searchers once again divided into groups while May and Bowen scanned the area above.[5] As May flew west, he caught sight of Johnson's distinctive snowshoe tracks. The pilot tried to spot the fugitive and, failing to do so, flew as low as he dared in an attempt to entice the outlaw to fire his gun, thereby revealing his location. The ploy did not work.

Monday, February 15, 1932

Dense fog rolled in, grounding the plane, but by afternoon the men on the ground were able to make some headway, and they found several places where their quarry had obviously made camp.

Tuesday, February 16, 1932

Fog continued to keep May and Bowen from flying, but a posse on the ground picked up fresh tracks heading west on a tributary of the Bell River known as Eagle River.

By now the difference between daytime and nighttime barely registered on the exhausted searchers. Given the nature of an Arctic winter, they would not have seen much sunlight anyway, but in the weeks since the hunt had started, when howling blizzards hadn't swept curtains of snow between them and the few hours of watery winter sunlight they might have had, fog had effectively blocked the sun's rays.

Just as fatigue forced an end to their search that day, Johnson's snowshoe prints were spotted once again. The searchers knew they were gaining on him, because these tracks were less than a day old. Tomorrow could be the last day they had to endure this mind- and bone-numbing chase through some of Earth's harshest conditions.

Even an elder from a nearby village predicted that the trapper known as Albert Johnson would not live to evade the police for one more day. It was important for the searchers to believe that, because they knew they were weakening. Chunks of ice encrusted their beards, their parkas and mitts were frozen stiff, and they were thoroughly disheartened. How could it be that the man they were chasing had not dropped dead weeks ago from starvation or exhaustion or both?

Wednesday, February 17, 1932

Finally, 49 days after the manhunt had begun, conditions were perfect for searching, both on the ground and from the air. The fog had lifted and the wind had died down, allowing the temperature to rise somewhat, to a still-cruel -45°c.

The men loaded their rifles and broke camp early. At the rate they were gaining on him, it could be only a matter of hours before they'd catch sight of their quarry. Royal Canadian Signals Corps Sergeant Heps Hersey, a former Olympic athlete, directed his dog team to the lead. Special Constable Joe Verville's sled followed close behind. With three more men patrolling the riverbank on foot, the posse started up the frozen Rat River. Wop May's Bellanca droned in the distance, its two-way radio crackling with static.

Just before noon, driving his dogs as fast as he dared, Hersey rounded a sharp bend in the river. There, no more than 300 metres in front of him, was his target. Hersey dropped to one knee and shouted to Johnson, "This is your last chance to give yourself up," before aiming and firing his Lee Enfield rifle, desperately determined to bring the manhunt to an end.

Soon an exchange of gunfire echoed through the frozen air, bringing the rest of the posse running with guns aimed and firing. Seconds later, the deadly chase was over. The fugitive the lawmen had pursued for nearly seven weeks lay lifeless, face down on the frozen Eagle River.[6]

Sergeant Hersey had been critically injured. A bullet from Johnson's gun had passed through one of his lungs, collapsing it completely before nicking his other lung and his heart. He lay in the snow bleeding profusely and in tremendous pain.

Within minutes, May's plane appeared over the horizon. Flying low over the river, the pilot spotted Johnson's body and dipped the aircraft's wings to indicate that he knew the manhunt had ended and that he would attempt to land on the river. After making half a dozen touch-and-go passes over the frozen, snow-covered river in order to create a landing strip of sorts, May brought his plane to a halt.

The first order of business was to gently load Sergeant Hersey into the plane and fly the badly injured man the 201 kilometres to Aklavik, where assistant acting surgeon Dr. J. Urquhart was standing by. The flight took 45 stressful minutes. There is little doubt that without the combination of May and Bowen's skillful flying through nearly impossible conditions, the surgeon's abilities and that most valuable of assets— a bit of good luck—Hersey would have bled out and died that night. As it was, he went on to live a long and successful life, once mentioning in an interview that the only lasting effect from the Mad Trapper's bullet was that he had to significantly alter his golf swing.[7]

Millen's body was to be flown home to his family for burial. Before the plane left, the people in and around Aklavik—both military and civilian—gathered for a small ceremony to pay tribute to the constable. Then Wop May and Jack Bowen, accompanied by Constable Alfred King as an RCMP escort, loaded Millen's canvas-wrapped body into the Bellanca, a plane too small to hold a coffin, and flew to Edmonton, Alberta, where Edgar Millen Sr. was waiting to receive his son's remains. Constable Millen was buried in Edmonton with full military honours. A park in the northeast section of the city is named after him.

Albert Johnson's body and his burial received very different treatment. After the corpse was flown into Aklavik, Dr. Urquhart performed a complete autopsy, which included the creation of a detailed dental chart. Johnson's weight at death was found to be an emaciated 145 pounds (his weight when he was last seen alive was estimated to be about 170 pounds). He was not tall, and he had a stooped posture.

Above and on opposite page: Viewing these grisly post-mortem photographs makes it easy to understand why members of the posse who finally brought down the fugitive were later haunted by his striking image. His face forever frozen into a malevolent grin, even in death Johnson appears to be defiant. PHOTO COURTESY OF RCMP MUSEUM

(C O P Y)

Aklavik, N.W.T.,
February 20, 1932.

The Officer Commanding,

Description of albert Johns
from an examination made at
Aklavik, N. W. T. Feb. 20/93.*

man known as Albert ~~Johnson, from an examination~~
this date :

Height, 5 ft. 9 in. to 5 ft. 9½ in.

Chest, 34 inches.

Estimated weight, 145 to 150 pounds.

Light brown hair, beginning to recede on forehead,
light brown beard and mustache; beard and mustache
less than a month old.

Pale blue eyes, snubbed, up-turned nose; moderate
prominence of cheek bones; ears definitely lobed;
lows-set and close to head.

Small wort or mole, 2 inches to left of spine, mid
lumbar region; this is only natural mark on body.
There are no operation scars or evidences of old
fractures.

Apparent age, 35 to 40 years.

Teeth: Well cared for, numerous fillings, though obviously neglected for a period of some months.

Left upper jaw: Third molar and wisdom tooth extracted; silver filling second molar, gold filling second
incisor.

Right upper jaw: First molar extracted, also third molar
and wisdom tooth extracted. Second molar large cavity,
anterior surface where filling has dropped out, bicuspid
also extracted.

Left lower jaw: Second and third molars extracted.

Right lower jaw: Bicuspid crowned with gold to which
is attached gold bridge reaching back to third molar
which is also gold crowned; wisdom tooth extracted.

Feet approximately 9½ inches long.

I have the honour to be,
Sir,
Your obedient servant,

(Sgd)   J.A.Urquhart,

Acting Assistant Surgeon.

Dr. Urquhart, the region's coroner, filed this detailed post-mortem description of Albert
Johnson.

This memorial marked the site where Constable Millen died from a gunshot fired by the Mad Trapper. GLENBOW ARCHIVES NA-1685-4

Urquhart filed his findings with the authorities and placed Johnson's body in a cold-storage locker, no doubt hoping that a relative would step forward to claim it once they learned of his death. No one did.

The corpse was reviled by the people of Aklavik. The town's coffin-maker outright refused to build a box that would hold the remains of a criminal who had killed such a respected police officer as Constable Millen. After completing all the medical and legal paperwork, Urquhart called upon his own employee, a handyman named Joseph Greenland, to build a plain, oblong box large enough to hold the corpse.

By mid-March, when no valid claim to the remains had been filed, Dr. Urquhart and the RCMP began making arrangements to take the corpse from its cold-storage locker and bury the Mad Trapper once and for all. It seemed like a straightforward plan, and the Anglican minister, Reverend Murray, approved. But even in death, the unidentified fugitive continued to cause controversy. Most people in the hamlet of Aklavik did not want his body sullying their cemetery, and they signed a petition toward that end. Eventually a compromise was struck. It was agreed that the body could be placed in an unconsecrated corner of the graveyard and buried by Greenland, who did so only because his employer had told him to.

While Joseph Greenland's carpentry skills were more than adequate to build the coffin, getting the frozen corpse to fit into the rough wooden box proved to be a considerable challenge. Johnson's body was frozen into an odd position, with its legs askew. The only way to get the coffin lid to close was to jump on it until the Trapper's frozen leg bones broke and collapsed to the bottom of the hastily constructed box.[8]

The burial of Albert Johnson marked the end of Canada's great Arctic manhunt, an event not without firsts. The Canadian government had set a precedent in granting permission for an aircraft to be used in the pursuit of a criminal. Sales of radios, largely viewed as mere novelty items until then, suddenly soared in North America and abroad. Throughout the manhunt, taxi drivers in New York and other busy centres had annoyed potential customers by refusing to take fares because they were too busy listening to hourly radio news bulletins about the chase. Just one hour after the fatal shootout on Eagle River in Canada's Northwest Territories, listeners around the world breathed a collective sigh of relief when they heard that the Mad Trapper had been fatally wounded, and then shuddered to learn that when his body was turned over, Johnson's lips were pulled back, frozen into an eerily sardonic grin.

Constable William Carter's report on the manhunt

Constable William Carter, who had been with the posse for the last weeks of the manhunt, was asked to write a detailed report of his experience. There are two major differences between the information he supplied in that report and the information given in the official report by Inspector Eames. Constable Carter stated that Johnson's cabin had not been destroyed by the dynamite charges, that it had barely been damaged. More important, he maintained that the Natives had lied to the RCMP about Johnson's interference with their traps. According to Carter's report, Johnson had waved a gun at the Natives when they had knocked on his cabin door in anticipation of a visit.

WARRANT TO BURY.

CANADA :
Northwest Territories.

To ....the R. C. M. Police, Aklavik, N.W.T.., xxxxxxxr,
and to all others to whom it may concern.

WHEREAS an inquisition hath this day been held upon view of the body of...
.............................Albert Johnson...
who, ...came to his death from bullets fired by a Police posse ....
while endeavouring to effect his arrest for the wounding of
Constable A.W.King and the murder of Constable E.Millen,
both of the R.C.M.Police
and now lies dead in ...the R.C.M.Police Guardroom at Aklavik, N.W.T............

"THESE ARE THEREFORE TO CERTIFY, that you may lawfully permit the body of the said.............
.........................Albert Johnson..
to be buried; and for your so doing this is your warrant.

GIVEN under my hand and seal this ....18th...................day .February. 19 32

....
Coroner, Northwest Territories.

N. W. T.
40.

The day after Johnson's death, Dr. Urquhart submitted this warrant to bury him.

We, The undersigned residents of Aklavik and District request
that the remains of Johnson whom as per the findings of the
Coroner's Jury was a murderer be buried in non-consecrated
ground and outside the confines of the settlement available
Clergy having justly refused to officiate at any form of
funeral ceremony.

[signatures]

Obtaining permission to bury Johnson's body proved to be complicated. The people
of Aklavik did not want his body in their cemetery, so they organized a petition to stop
the burial.

Carter concluded his report by maintaining "the official [RCMP] report . . . is lax in detailing some of the incidents, and covers up many blunders. Inspector Eames, Corporal Wilde and myself held a lengthy conference sometime after the conclusion of the case and, I presume, before the official report was forwarded 'outside.' Each event was discussed and *the version* [Carter's emphasis] to be adhered to when discussing the case with the public was impressed upon me. I was also informed that it would not be necessary to report on my part in the matter as Inspector Eames would cover the entire case. At that time I did not inform Inspector Eames that my instructions were to report personally to the Officer Commanding in Edmonton, who was also in command of the Mackenzie area; I was to provide a verbal account of the affair, as he suspected some inefficiencies of organization and co-ordination of personnel employed in the 'hunt.'"

Very soon after the Mad Trapper manhunt, Inspector Eames sent Constable Carter on "to take charge of Arctic Red River Detachment," which meant Carter's report "did not reach the Officer Commanding in Edmonton until the first summer mail plane." This in turn meant Carter's official report reached headquarters "later than Inspector Eames' official report, so that the official version was therefore the one accepted by the Force and subsequently by newspaper and magazine editors."

Mystery Man

AND SO THE MOUNTIES, WITH substantial assistance, had their man. But who *was* this man? Attempts to identify Albert Johnson began immediately. The RCMP sent copies of the dead man's fingerprints to both Canadian and American police. As a result, wardens of jails dotted around the United States and Canada wrote to the RCMP with descriptions of escapees, and various police departments offered leads. Social agencies asked for descriptions of the dead man in hopes that he would turn out to be a recipient they could strike from their rolls. A dentist in California asked for copies of Johnson's dental records, perhaps thinking they might belong to one of his patients.

As word of the fugitive's death spread, more and more people responded. Claims began to trickle in from people maintaining that they had a right to the $2,410 cash, the poor-quality pearls and the alluvial gold that had been in Johnson's possession at the time of his death. No one claimed the corpse, although many people inquired about it. Lawyers sent letters on behalf of clients claiming to be related to the

Opposite: In January 1940, some of the items from Albert Johnson's estate were transferred to the RCMP Museum in Regina, Saskatchewan. Eventually, most of the RCMP documents about the case were transferred to Library and Archives Canada in Ottawa. The rest of the "valueless" effects found with Johnson were apparently thrown into the Ottawa River. (Concern for the environment was obviously not big in those days.) None of the items clarified Johnson's identity or background. In fact, some added to the mystery. Where would he have acquired pearls?

ROYAL CANADIAN MOUNTED POLICE

Schedule

schedule as of 7 Feby 32

List of effects of Albert JOHNSON - Estate of

(a)　　Articles of value which it is considered should be
　　　　forwarded to The Public Administrator.

　　(1)　small glass bottle containing;-
　　　　　five pearls, approximate value $15.00 and five pieces
　　　　　of gold dental work 4 dwt. approximate value $3.20.

　　(2)　small glass bottle containing:-
　　　　　13 dwt. of alluvial gold, approximate value $9.36.

(b)　　Articles which it is requested be left with the
　　　　R.C.M.Police for inclusion in the R.C.M.Police
　　　　Museum at Regina, Sask.

　　(1)　Savage 30-30 Rifle, No. 293575, Model 99.
　　(2)　Ivor Johnson Sawed off shot gun, No. 5537XF. 16 ga.
　　(3)　.22 Winchester Rifle, Model 58, No number. Stock
　　　　　sawn off.
　　(4)　Pocket Compass.
　　(5)　Axe - Handle bearing bullet mark.
　　(6)　Sack containing lard tin and lid used as tea pail,
　　　　　showing bullet holes.

(c)　　Articles of no value, for which authority to destroy
　　　　is requested.

　　(1)　Knife made from spring trap.
　　(2)　Match safe.
　　(3)　Gillette Safety Razor.
　　(4)　Envelope containing piece of three cornered file;
　　　　　awl made from three cornered file; chisel made from
　　　　　nail.
　　(5)　Small knife made from piece of metal, with mooseskin
　　　　　cover.
　　(6)　Mooseskin Rifle Cover.
　　(7)　Mooseskin pouch.
　　(8)　Mooseskin sewing pouch containing needles and thread.
　　(9)　Small spring.
　　(10)　Nails wrapped in tinfoil.
　　(11)　Matches wrapped in tinfoil.
　　(12)　30-30 Cartridge box containing small empty bottle and
　　　　　piece of wax.
　　(13)　Sack containing thirty-nine 30-30 shells.
　　　　　　　　1 box .22 shells (50)
　　　　　　　　1 box .22 shells)30)
　　(14)　Seven pieces of moosehide.
　　(15)　Sack containing six empty sacks:
　　　　　　　　15 pieces of babiche.
　　　　　　　　1 large bundle of babiche. (showshoe lacing)
　　　　　　　　1 bdle Sewing thread.   N
　　　　　　　　1 piece mooseskin lace.
　　(16)　Calico rifle cover.
　　(17)　Large envelope containing:
　　　　　　　　1 box Pony Matches.
　　　　　　　　1 bdle Sulphur Matches wrapped in tinfoil.
　　　　　　　　1 bdle Sulphur Matches wrapped in paper.
　　　　　　　　1 tinfoil packet containing 2 pills.
　　　　　　　　1 paper package containing six pills.
　　　　　　　　1 paper package containing fish hooks.
　　　　　　　　1 tinfoil package containing oily rag.
　　　　　　　　1 leather cover containing comb and sewing materials
　　　　　　　　1 paper and tinfoil package containing grey powder.
　　　　　　　　1 rag bundle containing twine.

　　　　List of effects of Albert JOHNSON - (Con't)
　　　　---

　　　　1 rag bundle containing sewing twine.
　　　　1 paper package containing 24 pills.
　　　　1 paper package containing fish hooks.
　　　　4 ,22 Shells.
　　　　4 - 16 ga. Shot Gun Shells.
　　　　1 Moosehide folder containing mirror.
　　　　1 rag containing pepper.
　　　　1 sack containing salt.

Trapper, and women from all over North America wrote to the RCMP, claiming that Albert Johnson was their scoundrel of a husband who had deserted them and varying numbers of children. (One of the many letters received from the United States was addressed with only two lines: "Canadian Mounted Police, Montreal." Remarkably, the envelope made it through the system and reached the appropriate desk!) In October 1933, the Metropolitan Life Insurance Company wrote because a widow had filed a claim against Johnson's estate. The claim was denied.

Not everyone was after something. Some people wrote to tell the police that they were sure the deadly loner had been an American gangster known as the Blueberry Kid, whose real name was either Harry Bushnell or Al Johnson. Bushnell's height, however—he was known to stand roughly six feet tall and weigh more than 200 pounds—put him out of the running immediately. The coincidental alias "Al Johnson" therefore clarified nothing. The name of another gangster, Coyote Bill (William Banty), was also put forth and eventually rejected.

Others wondered whether the fugitive had perhaps been a miner attempting to protect a secret cache of gold. A number of people who have examined the case feel certain that the man the authorities chased and finally killed was simply someone visiting the Mad Trapper's cabin. This theory seems to have been created decades after the manhunt, as there are no indications from any reports filed in the 1930s that there was even the possibility of mistaken identity.

Besides circulating the Mad Trapper's fingerprints and dental records, the RCMP made its own efforts to identify the mystery man, going so far as to examine Johnson's clothes to see whether they could be traced to any particular source. But nothing he was wearing "bore any distinctive marks"; the clothing could easily have been purchased at any "general store."

In the end, the only real clues the RCMP had about the fugitive's background, other than the descriptions provided by people who had encountered him in the months prior to the manhunt, came from his

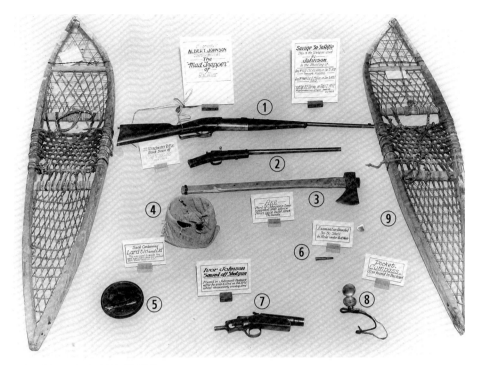

PHOTO COURTESY OF RCMP MUSEUM

The Effects of Albert Johnson

1. Savage 30-30 rifle used to kill Constable Millen and seriously wound Constable King and Sergeant Hersey

2. Winchester .22 rifle with stock sawed off

3. Axe (note bullet groove in handle)

4. Lard tin used for melting snow to make tea

5. Bullet-pierced lid of same lard tin

6. .30 shell found hidden behind the butt plate of the Savage rifle

7. Sawed-off Ivor Johnson shotgun

8. Pocket compass

9. Handmade snowshoes

The items pictured are on display at the RCMP Museum in Regina, Saskatchewan.

amazing survival skills and superb physical condition. These qualities suggested a background with extensive training, possibly with the military or a police force somewhere. (In fact, some men who contacted the RCMP were sure they had served in the military with Johnson.)

Although the number of inquiries dwindled over the years, they never let up completely. Even decades after the manhunt, the RCMP continued to receive letters from people who thought they might be related to the long-dead fugitive. All inquiries were followed up, and none were ever written off until it became absolutely clear that there was no similarity between the man known as Albert Johnson and the individuals the correspondents wrote about in their letters. The people described in those letters always proved to be too tall, too old or, in one case, too British. One was said to have spoken with a heavy Russian accent, which ruled him out as a candidate because people who had spoken to Albert Johnson, such as storekeepers, had always indicated that he'd spoken with a slight Scandinavian accent.

Not surprisingly, because the mystery of Albert Johnson's identity remained unsolved, many theories have been offered over the years. A number of the tales have become so romanticized that it is impossible to know where the facts leave off and conjecture begins. Even at the time of the manhunt, rumours circulated that the Mad Trapper was not a man at all, but a demon with superhuman strength and endurance.

Some stories have suggested that the Mad Trapper was actually a victim of sorts. According to an article that ran on March 17, 1932, in the *Courier*, a newspaper in Cranbrook, British Columbia, Albert Johnson was a man driven mad by the loss of his love:

> Two years ago, Johnson a quiet, taciturn trapper, married an Eskimo maiden . . . They lived in happiness until she left him to visit her people. She never returned.
>
> Johnson went out to visit her tribe, wondering why she was detained. She had not visited them, Eskimos told the man, and he set out to find her. Returning to his lonely cabin, he discovered the skeleton of his bride, who had died on the trail.

Broken hearted, he carried the remains to his cabin, where he lashed the bones together with deerskin thongs and clothed them in the finest furs he could find, even resorting to stealing furs from the traps of Indians. Complaints of the natives brought the Royal Canadian Mounted police to the scene.

Fearing that the policemen would interfere with the remains of his bride, the demented man seized his gun to drive them away.

It is interesting that this fanciful version of the story had evolved to include even the detail of interference with the traplines.

One of the earliest and better-known theories holds that "Albert Johnson" was in fact the alias of a man called Arthur Nelson, who was known to have been in the area several years earlier. This suggestion seemed plausible, because the dates are right and some of Nelson's mannerisms, and certainly his physical appearance, were similar to Albert Johnson's.

Arthur Nelson was first seen in the area of the Ross River post in the Yukon in August 1927. He was described as being about 5 feet 9 inches (152 centimetres) tall and weighing approximately 175 pounds (79 kilograms), with light-coloured hair and distinctive blue-grey eyes. He was notably round-shouldered. Although fluent in both English and Swedish, he rarely spoke, and when he did speak English, it was with a slight Scandinavian accent. The only information anyone remembered Nelson having volunteered about himself was that he had come from Wisconsin.

In June 1928, Nelson was back at Ross River post, where he bought a Savage 30-30 and some .22 shells. He was known to have camped the following winter near the south fork of the Stewart River. A trapper who claims to have spent the night at Nelson's cabin later reported that his host had told him he was of Danish origin.

Given the conflicting reports of his fluency in Swedish, the reference to his Danish origins and another alleged comment he had made about being Norwegian, it is difficult to accept any of these accounts as accurate.

Many are convinced that Albert Johnson and this man, photographed in 1927 or 1928 at the Ross River post and known around the area as Arthur Nelson, were one and the same. Even if this were true, it would not reveal much, because next to nothing was known about Arthur Nelson, either. PHOTO BY STERNWHEELER PILOT FRANK SLENI; COURTESY OF RCMP MUSEUM

The next time Nelson was seen was in April or May 1931 in Mayo, on the Stewart River in the Yukon, where he bought provisions, including a large supply of Beecham's pills. The Mad Trapper had a supply of similar pills with him when he died, but given that thousands of people all over the world faithfully took this patented "cure-all" medication, it is far from conclusive evidence that Johnson was in fact Nelson. After he bought the pills, Arthur Nelson was last seen in April or May 1931 around Keno, 465 kilometres north of Whitehorse in the Yukon.

On July 9, 1931, a few months after Arthur Nelson disappeared, a man calling himself Albert Johnson appeared in Fort McPherson, Northwest Territories. The men's similar physical characteristics (same approximate height, weight and posture) and Scandinavian accents have led many people to assume that Arthur Nelson and Albert Johnson were the same person—a theory that has never been disproved. Unfortunately, even if it were true, this theory does not reveal much, because no more is known about Arthur Nelson than is known about Albert Johnson. As a result, all the same questions remain. Where did the man come from? Where did he learn his marksmanship and survival skills? And why did he react so violently when Constable King knocked on his cabin door?

In 1932, no one had answers to those questions. The Great Depression soon had a stranglehold on the North American economy, and the

---

BEECHAM'S PILLS

One of the factors indicating a possible connection between the Mad Trapper and the man known as Arthur Nelson was a quantity of Beecham's pills. Given the popularity of this "medication" and the range of ailments for which it was recommended (these included constipation, headache, dizziness or swimming in the head, wind, pain and spasms of the stomach, bilious or liver complaints, sick headaches—presumably different than the headaches listed previously—cold chills, flushing heat, lowness of spirits and all nervous affections, scurvy and scorbutic affections, pimples and blotches on the skin, bad legs, ulcers, wounds, maladies of indiscretions, kidney and urinary disorders and menstrual derangements), it is perhaps only a coincidence and certainly not conclusive proof. Considering the stamina Johnson demonstrated, it seems safe to assume that his overall health was good.

public's interest in the strange and nearly unbelievable saga of Albert Johnson slowly waned, replaced by much more serious and personal concerns. As the years went by, and the body of the so-called Mad Trapper lay decomposing in its Arctic grave, Johnson's tremendous feats of endurance and the worldwide excitement he had generated during the last seven weeks of his life were forgotten by all but a few.

One person who had not forgotten about them was Wallace Rustad, a student at Minot State University in North Dakota who would go on to a long and illustrious career, including serving as chief of staff for two members of the United States House of Representatives and North Dakota senator Kent Conrad. But in 1962, Rustad was simply a student trying to find a topic for a history term paper.

"Professor Nels Manvel Lillehaugen wanted us to research and write on some matter of local history," Rustad told me in a telephone interview. So he set about investigating the disappearance of a local young man named Johnny Johnson around 1922.

While digging through archival files, Rustad came across the photograph of Albert Johnson that the RCMP had taken before the captured fugitive's burial. Acting on a hunch, he decided to show it to Petra Johnson, an elderly woman living in Grenora, North Dakota. With evident sorrow, she claimed that the picture was of her son, John Johnson, who had disappeared years before, during the early 1920s, after serving terms in several jails around the United States for an assortment of petty crimes.

With that kind of proof, Rustad felt confident he could finish his paper with the conclusion that Johnny Johnson and Albert Johnson were the same person.

Some years after Rustad wrote his term paper, Yukon author Dick North developed an intense interest in the man known as Albert Johnson. He subsequently spent decades attempting to solve the Mad Trapper mystery and writing books about it, the first of which was published in 1972. After a great deal of research, mostly without the assistance of the internet, North too connected Albert Johnson to Johnny Johnson. In addition to their physical resemblance, North found many other similarities between the two men.

Left: Some people believed Johnny Johnson, the man in this mug shot taken at Wyoming State Penitentiary, was Albert Johnson as a teen.
PHOTO COURTESY OF WYOMING STATE PRISON

Opposite page: Another theory was that "Albert Johnson" was another alias of Charles W. Johnson, who also called himself William Hoffner and John Johnson, pictured here a few years later at San Quentin Prison in California. His prison intake form lists his place of birth as "nowhere."
PHOTO AND DOCUMENTS COURTESY OF SAN QUENTIN PRISON

		Rem.			Rem.			Rem.				
Height	1 m 7 6 8		Head lgth.,	1 9 0		L. Foot	2 7 0		Color of Left Eye	Circle,		Age 28 Years
Outs, A.	1 m 7 7 0		" width,	1 5 2		" Md F	1 2 2			Periph, Z	Blue	
Trunk,	9 3 5		" lengh.,	5 7		" L F	9 8			Pecul.		Born in Colorado
						" F	4 7 3					

			Finger Print	11 R I o 19	Finger Print	
English	5 9 3/8		Classificaion	4 – o o 17	Reference	
Heigh						

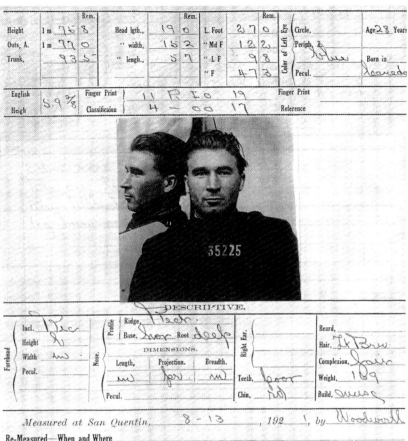

35225

DESCRIPTIVE.

Forehead	Incl. Rec.	Nose	Profile	Ridge, Flesh.		Right Ear		Beard,
	Height			Base, mex Root deep				Hair, Dk Brn
	Width med.		DIMENSIONS.					Complexion, fair
	Pecul.		Length,	Projection.	Breadth.	Teeth, poor		Weight, 189
			med	prv.	med	Chin, rd		Build, medus
			Pecul.					

Measured at San Quentin, 8 - 13 , 192 1 , by Woodworth

Re-Measured—When and Where _____

Institution CALIFORNIA STATE PRISON.   Reg. No. 35225

NAME Charles W Johnson 3 T   Color white

Alias _____   Received 8-13-21

County Lassen   Sentence 1 – 10

Crime Grd Larc.   Disch. _____

Occupation Machinist   Paroled _____

Previous Record As Wm Hoffner #2210 Rawlins, Wyo 14½
mo. Larc Disc. Aug 4-1916 – As John Johnson
#5267 Deer Lodge, Mont. 3 to 9 yrs. Robbery
Paroled 4-6-18

Num. Order	MARKS, SCARS AND MOLES
	2 dim scars rt s fhd.
	Blo. scar lo lft in
	Brn Bthmrk cent fhd
	Lrg burn scar lo rt in at elb.

Over the years, the Trapper's gravesite in the Aklavik cemetery has been marked by a series of signs. PHOTO FROM HERITAGE HOUSE COLLECTION

In *The Mad Trapper of Rat River: A True Story of Canada's Biggest Manhunt* (2003), North describes how Johnny Johnson was born in Norway during the late 1800s, immigrated to North America as a child with his family and left the family farm in his early twenties, ostensibly headed to Canada but never contacting his family again. North concluded that Johnny Johnson of Grenora, North Dakota, was the man who had come to be known as the Mad Trapper.

Over the years, as more and more people read North's books, the strange-but-true story from the Arctic gradually made its way back into the public's awareness. And despite North's conclusion, all the old questions resurfaced. The mystery of the Trapper's true identity remained.

New myths and legends grew up around the facts (such as they were) and led to the production of books, poems, songs and films. Modern-day versions of the story were examined frequently—and occasionally enhanced.

But with the discovery of DNA and the role that DNA matching plays in modern-day forensic investigations, there was at last a possibility that someone could solve the mystery. Michael Jorgensen and Carrie Gour hoped that they, using these tools, would be the ones to do that.

The Aklavik cemetery, with its plain
white markers, is a modest one.
PHOTO BY MATTHEW SPIDELL

PART **TWO**

A **New Approach** to Solving an **Old Mystery**

WHEN MICHAEL JORGENSEN AND Myth Merchant Films decided to try to solve the 75-year-old mystery of the Mad Trapper's true identity through DNA testing and then broadcast both the process and the results in a television documentary, he knew he faced a hurdle that no one to date had cleared. He would need the Aklavik community's official approval to exhume Albert Johnson's body, approval that had been denied to previous investigators. One of the most credible exhumation requests had come in 1981 from author Dick North, who had been pursuing the mystery for decades. He wanted to compare Albert Johnson's fingerprints to those of Johnny Johnson, to prove his claim that Johnny and Albert were one and the same person. However, North's request was denied.

Jorgensen, too, was initially unsuccessful in obtaining permission. It wasn't until he and Carrie Gour sought the expertise of experienced community consultant Mel Benson that there seemed to be any hope of initiating the project they envisioned. With his worldwide business and negotiation background, Benson brought a unique and, as it turned out, critically necessary combination of skills to the table. Benson was highly respected for his work in northern Canada with Imperial Oil, winning a 2003 National Aboriginal Achievement Award for Business. Chief Charles Furlong of the Aklavik Indian Band and Aklavik's mayor, Knute Hansen, knew Benson well, and he had their well-deserved trust. These factors were pivotal. Without them, it's unlikely that the film project would have gone ahead.

Benson accompanied Jorgensen and Gour on several trips to Aklavik to work on gaining the community leaders' understanding and support for the documentary they hoped to make. Dennis Allen, an Aboriginal filmmaker from Inuvik who was very keen on the project, also joined the trio.

Gour had grown up in the western Arctic. Because of her long, close association with the area and her fondness for its people, she took on the job of visiting as many members of the community as she could, going door-to-door. During her interviews, it became obvious that some residents, unlike Albert Johnson's contemporaries, empathized with Albert Johnson, feeling that over the years they too had effectively been chased away from their land and that their freedom to live their lives as they chose had been threatened.

Everywhere she went, the determined filmmaker stressed that the exhumation would be conducted in a completely respectful manner. She explained that it would take place in the privacy of a tent, that blessings would be offered before and after the disinterment and that the body would not be taken anywhere or even seen by anyone who did not need to see it. As the residents of Aklavik realized that the exhumation process might provide a family somewhere with answers about what had happened to a loved one, the tide of opposition began to recede. Many people in town mourned for relatives who over the years had left home, never to return. In the end, an amazing 70 percent of the population approved of the identification project. One of the most compelling reasons for the community's support was that the project acknowledged the crucial contribution these people's ancestors had made in capturing the Mad Trapper. Without the specialized knowledge of the Aboriginal members of the search party, there is little chance the RCMP could even have survived the chase, let alone succeeded.

The cemetery in Aklavik is a hive of activity for several days before the dig begins. Everyone in the hamlet stops by at some point. PHOTO BY MATTHEW SPIDELL

THE MAD-T

ALBERT JOHNSON AR

AUG, 21,1927 COMPLAINTS O

BROUGHT THE RCMP. ON HIM

FICERS AND BECAME A FUG

WITH HOWLING HUSKIES, DA

FROZEN NIGHTS, THE POSSE

UP WITH HIM, HE WAS KILLE

RIVER, FEB, 17, 1932

On February 17, 2007, 75 years to the day after the Trapper was shot, the involved parties held a discussion not far from his gravesite and came to an agreement. It was a rare meeting of bureaucracy, curiosity, concern and science. Canada's ultimate cold case moved a step closer to being solved.[9]

Jorgensen and Gour's initiative, along with Benson's negotiation skills, had clearly created an atmosphere of mutual understanding and trust about the exhumation that had not existed during previous negotiations with the community. Myth Merchant Films came away with the community's tentative permission to exhume the body for the purpose of gathering specimens to be used in DNA analysis. At last, it seemed, there might be a chance to finally identify the remains buried in the northern hamlet of Aklavik.

But just when everything seemed to be moving ahead smoothly, one of the stories that had grown up around the legend of the Mad Trapper reared its head and slowed the process nearly to a halt. It seemed that around the time of Albert Johnson's capture, two suicides had occurred in the area. Because digging graves that far north in the winter was no easy feat, and because the bodies of suicide victims had had to be buried away from the main part of the cemetery, a well-respected Aklavik elder named Annie Gordon worried that there might be as many as three bodies in the grave designated for exhumation: Albert Johnson's, in his roughly made coffin, and those of the two suicide victims, whose bodies, Gordon recalled, had not been placed in coffins at the time of burial but merely wrapped in canvas shrouds.

If Gordon was right, and the team found any evidence of more than one body, the dig would have to be stopped immediately and completely, as the registrar general had given permission for the remains of only one human being to be disturbed.

With this caveat on their minds, Jorgensen and Gour began to assemble a "dream team" of experts to work at the cemetery on the day of the exhumation and conduct follow-up investigations. It was not going to be a straightforward endeavour, so the producers knew they needed the involvement of leading forensics experts with specialized skills for the project to succeed.

Only one day was allowed for the dig. Since time was going to be of the essence, the body had to be located quickly and accurately, so the scientists could apply their expertise. Although Albert Johnson's grave was marked, the marker had been changed over the years, the ground had shifted, and the layout of the cemetery had been altered. The film-makers hoped to find someone with knowledge of a technology that could be used to locate the coffin before the team started to dig.

This would be especially important if the story about the suicide victims being buried with the Trapper proved to be true. The film-makers needed to be absolutely positive that the correct body was selected for analysis. Considerable decomposition was suspected, so facial recognition would not be possible and the scientists would have to rely on what bones or teeth remained.

Once the correct body had been located and identified, specialists in DNA procedures would need to gather samples for running comparison tests later, and take them back to their labs for testing. To help develop a set of criteria for determining whether someone claiming to be a relative was a likely enough candidate to have his or her DNA tested, other experts would be necessary, to confirm Albert Johnson's approximate height and age and to determine any other potentially useful identification information not already known about the Mad Trapper.

Jorgensen and Gour began their search for team members by investigating various departments at leading universities. Soon they had compiled an impressive list of qualified scientists. Whether those people would be interested and available, however, was another matter. After all, these were experts whose skills were in great demand. To Jorgensen and Gour's delight, all of the scientists they approached agreed to work on the project, arranging their schedules accordingly once a date for the exhumation was determined.

During the film team's initial discussions, the first name that had come up was that of Dr. Owen Beattie, a forensic anthropologist who teaches and researches at the University of Alberta in Edmonton. He is frequently called upon to analyze human remains, often no more than bones. Beattie's name became a household word in the late summer of 1981, when he discovered the bodies of members of the Franklin Expedition, explorers who had perished in Canada's Arctic in 1845. Beattie has also worked for the United Nations in investigations of mass disasters, warfare and crimes against humanity.

The filmmakers believed Beattie's understanding of how human remains decompose in different locations and circumstances would be useful in attempting to identify Albert Johnson. His specialized knowledge could confirm whether the body in the Mad Trapper's grave met the expected criteria for a corpse that had been interred in permafrost for 75 years. Beattie could also remove bone specimens to examine at his lab and use them to create an osteobiography, or biography of the bones, which can provide clues about a person's circumstances in life, at death and even after.

Beattie would try to calculate how long the body believed to be that of Albert Johnson had been buried, and supply an approximate age at death for the body in that grave, its physical stature in life, information about possible ancestry and whether the skeleton contained any unique markings such as broken bones. All of these factors would then be compared to data about missing persons.

Another key member of the exhumation team was Dr. Sam Andrews, a forensic pathologist based in Calgary, Alberta. He investigates and conducts autopsies in cases of sudden and unexpected deaths in order to determine their causes. He is frequently called upon to serve as an expert witness in legal matters and court cases.

Because Albert Johnson's teeth might be all that remained of him, forensic odontologist Dr. David Sweet was enlisted. A dentist who studies the structure, development and abnormalities of teeth, he is also a world leader in DNA analysis and matching.

Sweet would use the 75-year-old dental records created just before Albert Johnson was buried in March 1932 to confirm that the body was

Forensic pathologist Sam Andrews (left) and forensic anthropologist Owen Beattie (centre) chat with film producer Dennis Allen. PHOTO BY MATTHEW SPIDELL

that of Albert Johnson. Each person's teeth and dental treatments such as fillings, bridges and extractions are unique, so Sweet would quickly be able to confirm that the body unearthed was beyond any doubt the one everyone was seeking, and then collect the samples for generating a DNA profile. With this profile, Sweet would be in an excellent position to evaluate samples supplied by people claiming to be related to Johnson. Because of the length of time the body had been buried, there were some serious concerns about the quality, and therefore the accuracy, of the DNA that would be extracted.

The other team member with an interest in the Mad Trapper's teeth was Dr. Lynne Bell, a forensic anthropologist and professor in the School of Criminology at Simon Fraser University in Burnaby, British Columbia. She is one of a few people in the forensics field who specialize in the analysis of tooth enamel to determine the region in which an individual may have lived during his or her youth. Using this new and experimental technique, Bell would analyze oxygen, carbon and nitrogen values in the enamel of the recovered teeth. Because adult teeth form during childhood, and bone represents the last 15 to 18 years of a person's life, readings of the teeth and bones can be taken to map out a person's distant and more recent past, including how well nourished they were and where they lived. For the purposes of tracing the Mad Trapper's relatives, this information would be extremely helpful, because if a candidate's family came from a part of the world excluded by Bell's findings, that candidate could be ruled out before going to the expense of DNA testing.

Because there were only post-mortem photos of Albert Johnson, Jorgensen and Gour wanted to create a visual representation of what the mystery man would have looked like at the time of his death. This desire led them to John Evans, program manager, North and West Regions, at the Canadian Police Research Centre in Edmonton. Evans would use what remained of the corpse's skull to collect the data necessary for a facial-reconstruction artist to create a computer-generated, three-dimensional likeness of what the Trapper might have looked like when he was alive. When prospective relatives presented photographs of the ancestor they believed might be Albert Johnson, the team could compare them with the images generated. A ballistics expert, Evans would also examine the bullet wounds on the body.

Finally, Matthew Spidell, a medical photographer who worked with Dr. Andrews in Calgary, would record the procedures performed on the day of the dig, as well as the biological evidence that would be unearthed. His photographs would become important records.

Based on the skills and experience of these top forensics experts, Jorgensen and Gour had every confidence that they had assembled the best team possible and felt prepared to proceed with the next step of their ambitious project.

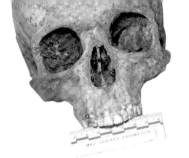

The **Exhumation** Begins

THERE HAD BEEN MUCH ACTIVITY around Johnson's gravesite in the days before the exhumation. The film crew had been on site for several days, and the hamlet of Aklavik had graciously hosted the people working to set the stage for the big day.

One of the people who arrived early was James Harrison of Maverick Inspection, an Alberta firm that specializes in ground-penetrating radar (GPR) surveys. He arrived in Aklavik on August 10, 2007, assigned the task of pinpointing the location of the coffin.

Harrison ran one of his high-tech instruments over the general area in which the coffin was believed to be buried. It was not long before the machine displayed a reading. There, not far below the surface of the ground, in almost exactly the place the coffin was presumed to be lying, was an oblong anomaly. What luck! Surely this had to be the coffin. It was the break Michael Jorgensen had been hoping for. Perhaps digging up the coffin would go as easily as finding it had.

Late that afternoon, Harrison took a 20-minute flight back to Inuvik, where the forensics experts would be assembling that evening at the Nova Inn. He was confident that his obligations for the project had been met, and fully expected to fly home to Alberta the following day. Jorgensen stayed at the gravesite in Aklavik to supervise the team of local workers he had hired to unearth the coffin. Meanwhile, Gour was at the Inuvik airport to greet and transport the members of the

James Harrison (left) searches with ground-penetrating-radar equipment until he detects a coffin-shaped anomaly exactly where the Mad Trapper is thought to be buried.
PHOTO BY MATTHEW SPIDELL

forensics team and me to the Nova Inn after our four-hour flight from Edmonton.

The first order of business after getting settled into our hotel rooms was to have a meeting over dinner and discuss plans for the following day—dig day. We all knew we had just one day to accomplish our task: the official permission was for August 11 only.

Excitement brimmed as we took over one of the banquet rooms at the nearby Mackenzie Hotel. The scientists were full of enthusiasm, and some were eager to renew acquaintances, having worked together on other projects. They also needed to exchange information and ideas about how to proceed the next day in Aklavik. Gour welcomed the team and stated that Myth Merchant Films was not only grateful, but also humbled to have so many great minds come together on the project.

While everyone was in a good mood, James Harrison was especially upbeat. Having spent a sizeable portion of the day operating his radar equipment at the Aklavik cemetery, he was feeling somewhat tired,

The probable location of the grave, as determined by ground-penetrating radar, is marked with yellow pegs, ready for the film crew to record the excavation. PHOTO BY MATTHEW SPIDELL

but mostly elated. When he addressed the group, he assured us that the machine he had used had done a wonderful job of locating the coffin. No one was surprised to learn that the radar had detected a dark, oblong shape directly under the sign that for years had identified Albert Johnson's grave. What else could it be except the coffin?

Harrison's excitement and sense of accomplishment were contagious. We all wished we could fly to the gravesite right after dinner, rather than having to wait until the following morning. As we left the banquet room, I teased Harrison that his exuberance had better not lead to any noisy partying that might disturb the scientists, as they would need their sleep for the demanding day ahead of them.

Ironically, Harrison did not sleep much that night, but it wasn't due to partying. At 1:30 a.m., his phone rang. It was Michael Jorgensen, calling from the cemetery with bad news: the site Harrison had mapped out with his sophisticated X-ray equipment had so far yielded nothing. At 5:00 a.m., the crew at the cemetery called again, advising him to cancel his flight home. Harrison needed to bring his equipment back to Aklavik and start all over again.

And so, while all was jubilant in Inuvik as we enjoyed our dinner and then turned in for the night, the frustration had been building in Aklavik. The team of people at the gravesite had been digging for hours and had reached roughly four feet below the surface—well below the spot Harrison's machine had indicated. Yet they still had not found anything, although it certainly was not for lack of effort. "By 1:00 a.m. we called in a backhoe and operator," Jorgensen recalled. "Around 2:30 a.m., the backhoe broke and sprayed hydraulic fluid all over, so we just went back to digging with shovels for the rest of the night. We took it in shifts, like we were playing hockey. We'd each shovel as hard as we could for as long as we could, till we couldn't go any longer. Then the next guy would jump in and repeat the process. We were at it for hours."

Some of the men who worked so hard during the night-long dig did so only out of kindness; they were not even members of the film crew. Philip Ross, a man known locally as an itinerant trapper, had "been working like a machine" throughout the night, according to Jorgensen, and had repeatedly declined Jorgensen's offers to make him a meal. "He said that he was determined to be the one who found the coffin," said Jorgensen.

"It takes a trapper to find a trapper," Ross had explained before grabbing a shovel and getting to work.

The height of the summer sun made it difficult to get a feel for the time of day or night, which was probably a blessing to this modern-day posse: they needed all the working light they could get. Even so, they were still up against the clock. As the coordinator of the dig, Jorgensen had tried to ensure that the coffin would be found before the rest of the exhumation team arrived.

But when morning came and the tired crew had not found the coffin, everyone knew there was a serious problem. What had looked so promising to James Harrison on the screen of his ground-penetrating radar machine had turned out to be nothing more than a rectangular-shaped "bubble" of permafrost. Despite the team's supposed high-tech advantage, the Mad Trapper was proving to be as elusive 75 years after his death as he had been when he was alive: there simply was no coffin buried in the spot indicated by Harrison's equipment.

In Inuvik, we were awake and waiting to fly to Aklavik to open the coffin we were certain had been unearthed by now. When Jorgensen called Gour by satellite telephone with the news—or non-news—from the cemetery, she was justifiably worried. Without a body, they would have no story.

Back at the graveyard, more than half a dozen members of Myth Merchant's production crew were on hand, ready and waiting with their expensive recording equipment for the coffin to be found. They were looking for a sign of something, *anything*, that would suggest the documentary team was not wasting its time.

Dennis Allen, who had worked through the night with the others, said their lack of success in finding the coffin had left the men who had worked so hard "feeling defeated."

After hours of digging, the exhausted and discouraged group realizes it is not going to find a coffin in the place indicated by the radar equipment. PHOTO BY MATTHEW SPIDELL

Inuvik film producer Dennis Allen is an invaluable resource during the days leading up to the dig and at the gravesite. He consults a local elder about the location of the coffin, ensuring that the project does not fail. PHOTO BY MATTHEW SPIDELL

Itinerant trapper Philip Ross works tirelessly through the night, motivated by his determination to be the one to find the coffin. PHOTO BY MATTHEW SPIDELL

James Harrison hoped to change that. As soon as he arrived in Aklavik with the rest of us who had spent the night in Inuvik, he began reworking the ground he had gone over so extensively the day before. The radar equipment identified a new location, and the night crew resumed the dig. Soon the scientists picked up shovels and began to help, but still there were no results.

Allen and the half-dozen local men who had been hired to help excavate gradually realized they needed to know more about the changes that had occurred in the decades since the Mad Trapper had been buried. But because nearly 75 years had passed, it seemed unlikely that anyone who might have witnessed the burial would still be alive to ask about it.

But Allen had an idea. Unnoticed, he left the tent and walked away from the cemetery, heading for Aklavik's Joe Greenland Home for Elders. He felt the only hope for success in this modern-day mission was the knowledge one of its residents might hold.

At the home, Allen began asking residents if any of them remembered the day the fugitive had been buried. Mary Kendi, then in her 90s and one of Alavik's most respected Gwich'in elders, told Allen that she remembered seeing the burial. Rather than try to explain where the coffin had been placed, she asked for a pencil and a piece of paper. Moments later, she had produced a rough map. According to legend, the coffin had been buried between two trees. Kendi's drawing showed the grave as being *beside* the trees.

Allen returned to the cemetery armed with this new information. According to Mary Kendi's small drawing, the Mad Trapper's coffin lay directly beneath the spot where the searchers had been piling the dirt they had removed during their hours of fruitless digging. The irony of this setback was not lost on anyone.

Philip Ross immediately set to work shovelling the freshly dug soil aside in order to get at the plot of solid ground they now needed to dig through. Ross' utter faith in the elder's word may have come from his First Nations heritage, or perhaps he was just not one to be easily discouraged. Either way, his drive to action seemed renewed.

And his efforts paid off. At last, all of us gathered in the tent heard the sound we had been hoping for: the distinctive dull thud that the metal blade of a shovel makes as it hits wood. Mary Kendi's memory had been exactly correct. The coffin was found less than a metre below the surface of the ground, just above the frost line. The body that had created so much misery and mystery for so many people over the years was finally within reach.

Once the coffin is opened, the remains will be laid out, examined and photographed on this specially constructed light table.

PHOTO BY MATTHEW SPIDELL

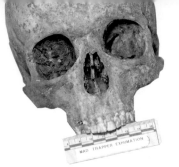

The Mad Trapper
Resurfaces

DESPITE THE ELATION OF THE find—or perhaps because of it—the huge tent we had been working in had become extremely hot and stuffy. Everything was damp; even the pages of notebooks were curling with the humidity. Knowing there were still hours of painstaking and difficult work ahead, Michael Jorgensen suggested that everyone leave the tent so the interior of the canvas shelter could cool down. This would allow us all to take a break and get some fresh air before the next long segment of the exhumation began.

As we filed out of the tent, Mel Benson checked his watch. It was 2:50 p.m. Several hours before, the experienced negotiator who had helped secure permission for the exhumation had assured me that the coffin would be found before three o'clock. Chief Charles Furlong had confided to me that a premonition of his had come true. "I knew they would find the body lying in an east—not west—direction," he said.

Grateful for a break, we all milled about, enjoying the cool, cloudy day. Some people gathered just outside the tent flap, while others made their way over to the band office, where some of the Aklavik residents had put out nutritious snacks and an assortment of drinks for us. Others wandered in contemplative solitude through the long grasses and grave markers of the cemetery. Everywhere, thousands of tiny mosquitoes buzzed about—but, oddly, did not bite.

After a while, as if on cue, we reassembled near the entrance to the tent. Sam Andrews commented that only after the coffin was found had the clouds cleared away and the sun come out. No sooner had he spoken than a magnificent eagle circled directly above us. The majestic bird swooped down and flew in a single circle directly over our heads before soaring higher and higher until it was out of sight. Its appearance seemed significant, and we all paused to appreciate its wild beauty. When we reconvened inside the tent, the air was fresher, and so were we.

Our shared anticipation was palpable. We approached the grave with a sense of excitement so strong you could feel it in the air. Despite the hours of tension when the coffin could not be located, it seemed we *were* going to have a chance to accomplish our mission in Aklavik. It took a few seconds for people's eyes to adjust to the light inside the tent, a strange combination of darkness punctuated harshly here and there by the film crew's lights. All eyes were on the exposed coffin, and as each of us became able to focus, a chorus of murmurs arose. We were all sure we could see something small and white lying on top of the coffin.

"Is that a bone?" someone asked, as Beattie stepped down beside the coffin. He picked up the white object and took a closer look at it.

"It's a bone, all right, but it certainly isn't a human bone," he said.

For a moment, there was a confused silence in the tent. Then John Evans stepped forward and took the bone.

"You'd better give that back to me," he deadpanned. "The dog I took it from will be looking for it."

The silence lingered a few awkward seconds, and then we erupted in laughter as we got Evans' joke.

Once the laughter had settled down, there were promises to keep before the coffin could be opened. As agreed upon prior to the exhumation, Aklavik's lay minister, Roxanne John, stood near the edge of the exposed grave and offered prayers for the soul of Albert Johnson, blessings he had not received when he was buried in March 1932. Although the cameras continued to roll, there was complete silence in the tent except for the words of prayer. You could tell everyone was taking a

The team is about to get its first glimpse of Albert Johnson's remains. The forensic scientists hope there will be enough of a skeleton left to test; the lay people in the group hope what is left will not be too gruesome.

PHOTO BY MATTHEW SPIDELL

The coffin lid has cracked and caved in from the pressure of the dirt that has covered it for more than 75 years. PHOTO BY MATTHEW SPIDELL

moment to remember what had happened so many years ago and to acknowledge what had already happened that day and was about to happen over the next few hours. The stillness held for a few moments after John's short service. Then we set to the tasks ahead.

Excitement simmered as Lynne Bell, Owen Beattie and Sam Andrews stepped down into the shallow pit to begin carefully scraping and brushing away the remaining dirt from the coffin. Compared with all the high-tech equipment around the tent, Bell's ordinary, small, red plastic dustpan seemed incongruous and almost comical.

The weight of the soil had caused the top of the coffin to sink below its sides, and for a few minutes there were concerns that there was no lid left at all. We breathed a collective sigh of relief when Beattie painstakingly probed around the edges of the wood and then stated with quiet assurance that he could follow the edge of the top. "The coffin's in good shape; the top's caved in a bit," added Andrews.

The wood had shrunk over the years, causing the coffin lid to crack and pull open near the middle. Slowly and carefully, the team pried sections of the lid from the sides of the coffin, until it was completely removed. Peering into the complete darkness within the box, it was easy to think the coffin was empty, that even in death Albert Johnson had eluded efforts to find him. But he had not, for there in front of us was a complete skeleton.

The bones were very black, and the flesh of his fingers had rotted away, leaving the fingernails to fall squarely onto the bones underneath. Despite the jostling of the earth's natural movement over the years and all the commotion of the dig in the past 24 hours, the fingernails had not been shifted. Aside from some strands of hair, the only soft tissue left on the Mad Trapper's skeleton were bits of leg muscle—evidence that the man who had led police on the gruelling manhunt 75 years before had indeed been incredibly strong. He'd had enough muscle tissue in his legs that it had not completely decomposed.

Albert Johnson's skull rested at an angle in the upper corner of the box. This was, no doubt, a result of the ground's inevitable heaving through seasonal changes over the decades, but it was not much of a stretch to imagine that the Mad Trapper was still looking over his shoulder, intent on eluding his pursuers.

Dr. Andrews noted that the degree of deterioration of the coffin and the remains were about what he had expected. Surprisingly, there was no smell beyond the moist, earthy aroma of freshly turned soil.

As Dr. Sweet gently lifted Albert Johnson's skull onto the light table that had been built specifically for this examination, debris fell from one of the eye sockets, and Dr. Beattie pointed out a tuft of hair that had not rotted away.

But it was not the hair that interested Sweet so much as the teeth. What he saw closely matched the dental chart drawn up prior to the fugitive's burial, which meant there was no question that we had the correct body.

Continuing his examination, Sweet noted that the teeth were worn. Albert Johnson had clearly not been to a dentist for some time, but apparently that had not always been the case. Sweet was surprised to find "very sophisticated dental work," which gave us our first clue about the Mad Trapper's identity. "This individual was from an upper socio-economic situation," Sweet said.

Dr. Bell was also interested in the Mad Trapper's teeth, but for a different reason—she would use one of them to create an oxygen map in her laboratory back in Burnaby, to help determine Albert Johnson's origins.

"What we've breathed becomes part of us, and part of the way we get oxygen is through the water we drink," she explained. The characteristics of water are different in various parts of the world, and this influences the makeup of our teeth.

Knowing where in the world Albert Johnson had grown up and lived would assist us in tracing his relatives. For instance, if someone believed they might be descended from the Trapper but their family came from a part of the world that contradicted Dr. Bell's findings, that candidate could be ruled out without our conducting DNA tests.

Lynne Bell (left) and Sam Andrews begin to investigate the bones, while Beattie (seated) takes notes. PHOTO BY MATTHEW SPIDELL

Owen Beattie (left) and Sam Andrews carefully brush away dirt from the skeleton; author Barbara Smith holds the light. PHOTO BY MATTHEW SPIDELL

The skull lays at such an angle that it appears the fugitive is looking back over his shoulder, watching for his pursuers. PHOTO BY MATTHEW SPIDELL

Historical accounts have stressed Albert Johnson's seemingly superhuman strength and endurance. That muscle fibres remain on his leg bones 75 years after his death is a definite indicator of the strength he had. PHOTO BY MATTHEW SPIDELL

Because the frigid Arctic climate had slowed the body's decomposition to the extent that Johnson's fingernails and some strands of hair remained, Bell hoped to deduce information about the man's diet by analyzing these valuable remains. She hoped this analysis would also reveal whether the Mad Trapper had been starving while he was being chased. Such knowledge might explain some of the fugitive's behaviour. For instance, had his mental capabilities been affected by starvation?

Patiently, the scientists removed the bones from the coffin, one by one, identifying each bone, enumerating it and then placing it onto a light table. After all the bones had been laid out, Beattie worked with Andrews to see whether the pathologist could get enough information from the skeleton to allow him to determine cause and manner of death. As the team's forensic anthropologist, Beattie made his own examination of the skeleton to determine the Trapper's approximate height, which involved measuring some of the bones and comparing their proportions.

The television cameras had not stopped for hours, but now, with the entire skeleton laid out on the light table, the scientists and medical photographer Matthew Spidell began taking detailed still photos. Cameras clicked, buzzed and whirred. The tent was a hive of activity: Beattie took samples and labelled them; Chief Charlie Furlong, who spent hours in the tent helping wherever he could, quietly bent down and pulled a protruding nail out of the coffin so no one would cut themselves on it; John Evans was busy helping anyone and everyone he could. Andrews took on the unenviable task of sawing the body's right femur in order to extract a specimen of bone marrow for DNA analysis by Sweet back in his laboratory at the University of British Columbia.

In addition to the complexity of the work, the sheer amount of it was considerable. But an air of professional cooperation developed quickly and held throughout the long day.

Evans' energy and tenacity in particular were valuable assets. Perhaps as a result of his years of police work, or perhaps simply because of his diligent nature, he worked tirelessly throughout the long exhumation process, helping with the actual digging and making himself available and useful to other members of the forensics team despite not having slept.

Just after 8:00 p.m., we took a break for dinner in the band office. At that point it was clear that the plane chartered to fly us back to Inuvik that night would have to be rescheduled for a later time. Nothing could stand in the way of completing the job we were there to do.

Discussions over dinner centred on how the dig was going and speculation about the end results. Sweet's indication that the Mad Trapper had once led a privileged existence introduced a new possibility. Had Albert Johnson been a remittance man, the son of a wealthy family in England or elsewhere in Europe who, initially at least, had received a regular allowance from home? Such a revelation might later remove some potential descendants from the running if their ancestors had been born into poverty.

After dinner we trooped back into the tent. Much work remained to be done. Aklavik residents dropped by the cemetery, naturally curious about all the activity in their usually quiet hamlet. However, for reasons of confidentiality and dignity, only those directly involved with the dig were allowed into the tent. But around 10:30 p.m., Aklavik's two RCMP officers were invited inside. Considering the enormous roles their predecessors had played in capturing the Mad Trapper, they had a special interest in the dig.

Throughout the long, intensely busy day and well into the evening, the atmosphere was remarkably quiet, positive and respectful. Still, as the hours passed, it was obvious that people were tiring. Gour brought cups of warm, sweet tea to help keep us going. Although it was nearly midnight, here in the Far North it was barely twilight, and youngsters were still out riding their bikes around the streets of Aklavik.

Finally the forensics experts concluded that their examinations were finished and they were ready to reinter the remains. Just as carefully as they had removed the bones from the rotting coffin, they laid them out again—this time in a new coffin that, once again, had been built specifically for Albert Johnson. Then, in an effort to preserve the integrity of

Odontologist David Sweet removes the jawbone for a detailed examination of the extensive and complex dental work in the Mad Trapper's upper and lower jaws.
PHOTOS BY MATTHEW SPIDELL

Finally, after hours of intensive examination, the skeleton is wrapped in a shroud and placed in a new coffin, along with the boards from the old coffin. PHOTO BY MATTHEW SPIDELL

the original grave, they placed the boards from the old coffin inside the new one, next to the skeleton. Once this was done, Roxanne John was brought back to the tent to offer prayers before the reinterment.

After the ceremony and reburial were over, a convoy of vehicles shepherded us to the Aklavik landing strip, where we boarded the plane that had been chartered to fly us back across the majestic Mackenzie Delta. It had been an incredibly full and tiring day for all of us, and our flights home were scheduled to leave 12 hours later. The work at the gravesite was complete, but we all had months of work ahead of us.

ADVANCING AKLAVIK

Following the exhumation, as a way of thanking the people of Aklavik, Myth Merchant Films made a cash donation to the hamlet. The residents put this money toward a plaque commemorating their community's involvement with the story of the Mad Trapper. They also built a new sign describing the events that took place from December 1931 to February 1932. It's constructed so visitors can pose behind it and be photographed as if they are part of the original manhunt.

Some of the remaining money was used to create a new website for Aklavik. Carrie Gour encouraged the community to establish "a marketing portal, a trading post of sorts," with an eye to residents' being able to promote their businesses and services, such as guiding, whaling and ice fishing, to people in other parts of the world. An added benefit of this part of the gift will be ongoing training of a group of citizens in the skills necessary for keeping the website current.

The strange, watery landscape of the Mackenzie Delta is our last view of the Aklavik area as we leave the site of the exhumation. PHOTO COURTESY OF MYTH MERCHANT FILMS

Lynne Bell examines one of the Mad Trapper's bones. Each one exhumed is examined from every angle. The scientists' examination results match Dr. Urquhart's autopsy findings that Albert Johnson was about 5 feet 9 inches tall and was in his mid-30s to early 40s. PHOTO BY MATTHEW SPIDELL

PART **THREE**

Forensics in the Field

IN THE SPRING AND FALL of 2008, Michael Jorgensen met with each of the scientists involved in the exhumation to discuss their individual roles and findings. These interviews were later used to create film clips and sound bites for the television documentary Myth Merchant produced for the Discovery Channel, entitled *Hunt for the Mad Trapper.* The following information comes from the transcripts of those interviews.

*   *   *

"I think every forensic pathologist would jump at the opportunity to be involved," said forensic pathologist Sam Andrews. "It's significantly different from what I do on a day-to-day basis. I've literally done a thousand post-mortem examinations, and to be able to do a post-mortem exam on an iconic Canadian legend, to help determine who the Mad Trapper was, is a once-in-a-lifetime experience I will never forget."

The circumstances of this particular post-mortem examination were completely unlike Andrews' usual exams—in this case, the cause of death was known, but a modern post-mortem observation had never been done.

Knowing he would be working inside a tent, hundreds of miles from his well-equipped lab, greatly increased the degree of difficulty for

Andrews. It was important that he plan for every eventuality. No one had any idea what condition the body would be in when it was finally unearthed, so even choosing what to include in his mobile autopsy suite was a challenge. However, the moment Albert Johnson's body was exposed, Andrews' enthusiasm for the project came to the fore.

"When the lid came off and I saw the skull, it was a different kind of feeling. I was kind of amazed at what we were doing," he said.

Of paramount importance was making sure the unearthed body was, in fact, Albert Johnson's. One of the identifying features Andrews would use was the way Albert Johnson's hair was said to grow in "tufts." To everyone's surprise, this feature was still evident.

"When we first removed the lid of the coffin, exposing the skull of the Trapper, I saw a tuft of blond hair, which I had seen in most of the photographs of the Trapper," Andrews recalled. "I thought this was surprising, and [this] reaffirmed that this was the body we were looking for. The injuries we saw in the left femur and the pelvis suggested that this individual was in a serious gunfight, which further confirmed that this was the individual we were looking for."

The conditions under which Andrews examined the Mad Trapper's skeleton were unusual, to say the least.

"When we finally were able to examine the body, it was late in the afternoon, further increasing the time pressures before we would have to reinter the body," he recalled. "It's unusual to be under significant time constraints when you're doing a post-mortem examination. As a forensic pathologist, [I] normally work under very controlled conditions. In a normal morgue, we are able to take as long as we need to do the most complete and thorough examination we require."

On August 11, 2007, in Aklavik, conditions were anything but normal. Time, facilities, tools and even adequate lighting were all in limited supply. But Albert Johnson's autopsy proceeded without a hitch.

Given that the body was buried in the 1930s in the Arctic, Andrews had expected it to be skeletonized—that is, reduced to a skeleton—but had not risked any further predictions about its condition.

Working with painstaking precision, Beattie and Andrews begin to remove the bones from the coffin, while author Barbara Smith keeps the coffin well illuminated. PHOTO BY MATTHEW SPIDELL

"He did have a little bit of tissue remaining on his lower extremities, on the thighs and buttocks area, which didn't totally surprise me because it does get quite cold up there," he said. "He did have a fair bit of hair and facial hair remaining, and most of his fingernails were present, which I didn't think we would recover.

"The soft tissue—things like muscle, connective tissue, skin—tends to start to decompose sooner than hair, for example. I was surprised to see the tissue, because it had been 75 years that he'd been buried. But things like cold will delay the decomposition process, so it wasn't a total surprise."

At the gravesite, certain points of identification related to the essence of the Mad Trapper began to emerge. People had always hypothesized that his odd stooped posture had developed because he was used to carrying heavy loads. Andrews found another reason for it.

"The Trapper had fusion of his sacral vertebrae, which are the last vertebrae near the pelvis. This fusion caused an angulation of the first sacral vertebrae toward the right, giving us the indication that he would have had some scoliosis. This could have led to chronic back pain," Andrews explained. "The [archival RCMP] report tells us that when the Trapper was shot and [killed] he had an approximately 150-pound pack on his back, which, with someone's back pain, would have caused further problems."

This revelation added another layer to the mystery by dispelling the common assumption that the Mad Trapper had done heavy work for most of his life, and it also supported a popular theory about the Mad Trapper—that Albert Johnson and Arthur Nelson could have been the same person. In large part, this theory originates from a shopkeeper's recollection that Nelson had purchased an unusually large supply of Beecham's pills, and the fact that Albert Johnson had had a supply of these pills with him when he was killed. These pills had intrigued previous investigators, and they interested Andrews, too, but not for the same reason.

"Kidney pills historically were marketed as treatment for back pain. I'm not sure how the name 'kidney pill' came about, but it was an analgesic medication similar to aspirin. The fact that these pills were found on the Trapper again supports our contention that he had scoliosis and some degree of back pain."

Andrews' examination of the skeleton also confirmed the long-standing legend about Albert Johnson's frozen body not fitting into the coffin that had been built for him, which stems from the coffin maker's son's remembering hearing the crack of breaking bones as men jumped on the wooden lid to get it to close.

"The fractures at the distal end [the end closest to the ankles] of the lower legs suggest to us that he had to be somehow wedged or pushed into the coffin," Andrews said. Clearly, those breaks had occurred after the Trapper's death.

Knowing people have always wondered how Albert Johnson was able to evade capture for so long, Andrews had also given thought to the daunting physiological challenges of the fugitive's survival during the 49 days he had been pursued through a mountainous area under Arctic winter conditions. "He was both physically and mentally strong, [in order] to elude the RCMP for weeks at a time in the cold Canadian Arctic. [It] took an incredible amount of stamina."

No matter how determined or motivated the Trapper might have been, though, a human body requires nourishment. "I'm not sure how he was able to eat and maintain his energy levels for the amount of activity he was doing," Andrews noted. "The normal caloric intake for an average male doing [normal] activity is approximately 2,500 calories per day. Now, the Trapper was running from law enforcement under severely harsh conditions—-40°c or -50°c—and would have needed a caloric intake four or five times what he would have required on a normal day. We know, based on the descriptions of his body when he was found, that he probably wasn't getting that caloric intake and most likely was starting to starve, based on the amount of activity he was doing."

The food Albert Johnson would have been getting certainly would not have provided anything approaching a well-balanced diet. He would also have had another, even greater requirement—hydration.

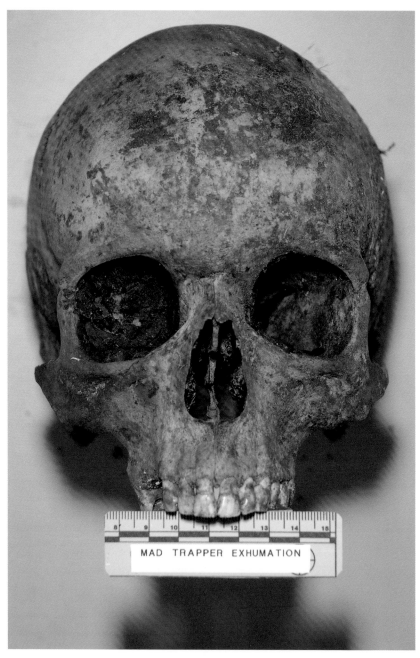

Knowing this will be their only chance to examine the Trapper's skeleton, the scientists take great care to document and record every aspect of the skull. PHOTO BY MATTHEW SPIDELL

Like other experts on the team, John Evans cannot do all of his work on site. Here he scans an image of Albert Johnson's skull into his computer so that he will have the necessary data to pass on later to a facial-reconstruction artist. PHOTO BY MATTHEW SPIDELL

"Breathing, and breathing heavily, when doing physical activity, you sustain [moisture] losses through your lungs, and he would have started to sweat. This [lost moisture] had to be replaced or he couldn't have continued on as he was," Andrews explained. "With the sweating, his clothes would have gotten wet, which could have resulted in problems with his body temperature, requiring more caloric intake."

Lack of sleep also would have reduced the Trapper's stamina over the course of the chase. Ultimately, Andrews could not offer an explanation for how or why the Trapper had survived for as long as he had under the conditions he had.

"That's part of the lore of the Mad Trapper. What he did over seven weeks in the Arctic—it's amazing to me. In essence, he was running a marathon every day, carrying a very heavy pack with, presumably, some back pain. It's hard to fathom doing this for as long as he did. In my mind, it's almost unbelievable. If it wasn't so well documented, I wouldn't have believed it. I don't know how someone could go on for as long as he did in those conditions. He would have had to have been very physically and mentally strong to go on for as long as he did—or perhaps he enjoyed the chase and eluding the posse coming after him, and that made him go on even longer."

*　　*　　*

Forensic anthropologist Owen Beattie recalled how none of the scientists had any way of knowing what would be lying in wait for them once the Trapper's coffin was opened. Even though it turned out that the coffin was actually not buried very deeply (just "80 centimetres below the surface . . . in a flood plain and a zone with some permafrost at variable levels," he recollected), the body could have conceivably been found in a coffin filled with air, soil or ice.

"[Prior to an exhumation], there are just too many variables," Beattie explained. "You can't really predict very scientifically exactly how the body is going to be, how it's going to appear or how well it's been preserved. It's totally related to the particular context. In removing the coffin lid, I guess I can say, [even though] this sounds strange, that I wasn't really surprised by what I saw, and yet I didn't expect to see what I saw."

He considered his first glimpse of Albert Johnson's skeleton personally significant.

"I'll remember that moment," he said. "Removing the coffin lid and seeing that there was a level of preservation. That was unexpected, for me. I just can't get beyond that, peeking into that shadow in there, and then with the lights, and seeing [the tufts of hair remaining] and being able to compare that directly with the photograph that was taken a day after his death. That was really quite remarkable."

Although Beattie was clearly heartened by the similarity between the hair on the skeleton and that in the drawing, he was also cautious about using it as a conclusive means of confirming that the body was the Trapper's.

"You can't use that as a positive identification, although it is an individualizing feature. [But] at that stage it was, in my mind—even before David Sweet was able to check the dentition for identity—indeed Albert Johnson. That was very satisfying, and I think the rest of the process started to unfold as it should."

As with any endeavour, there was a hierarchy in place within the scientific team. Beattie passed on the information he gathered to Andrews, who, as the team's pathologist, had "the authority to then develop an opinion on the cause and manner of death." Anthropologists, Beattie explained, formulate a professional opinion and make that available to other experts—in this case, to pathologist Andrews and forensic odontologist Sweet.

The challenge with exhuming Albert Johnson as a team, Beattie recalled, was to work out a method by which he and his colleagues could systematically examine the Mad Trapper's remains, to gain the information they each needed.

Completely engaged in her
work, Bell shines her light
over the skeleton.

"Dr. Sweet was anxious to begin his work on the skull, and John Evans [needed] to work on scanning the skull," Beattie recalled. This required removing the skull from the coffin, but only after the forensic anthropologist had examined it in context. Precision teamwork was required, and the way the scientific team gelled was a high point of the project for Beattie.

"We worked like clockwork! We all had our jobs to do, and it was a real team effort, and time just flew," he said. "I think we were able to, in the short period of time that we had at the site, get all of the information to allow a thorough and justifiable interpretation of the body and the context in which it was placed in the ground. Each one of us would see something that we recognized, and we brought that to the attention of the others. We would talk over our finding and look at the bone and that sort of thing, so we got a pretty thorough picture of [the Trapper's] physical state at the time he was killed."

Beattie was asked to determine the Trapper's approximate height by measuring some of the bones and comparing their proportions. He warned his colleagues that this method was "fraught with error and problems, [but] it can provide a reasonable estimate of how tall a person was." Beattie estimated the Trapper's height at just under 5 feet 10 inches, which was close to the original notes recorded by coroner Urquhart.

The Trapper's skeleton had additional stories to tell. Beattie determined that aside from some broken bones Albert Johnson had suffered earlier in his life, his skeleton looked very healthy, and the size of his musculature seemed average, not excessive.

"The bones provide an indication of approximate size of musculature. They can be robust or normal or gracile, that sort of thing. You can make that subjective determination." The almost complete absence of soft tissue made another approximation impossible. "If he was wearing pants we could have measured the waist, [but his clothing] was of course disintegrated, so we couldn't estimate how much he would have weighed."

Perhaps the single most astounding discovery Beattie made was that there didn't seem to be anything to indicate Johnson was malnourished.

Considering that he would have been living on berries and whatever small animals or birds he could have trapped and eaten raw, this particular finding amazed Beattie.

Age estimates passed down from people who interacted with Albert Johnson during the last months of his life suggest that he might have been somewhere in his mid-30s to early 40s. Dr. Beattie examined specific bones to come up with his own estimate of the Trapper's age at the time of death.

"The best bone we had for that is called the pubic symphysis," he explained. "It's where the two pubic bones come together at the front of the pelvis. Evidence there suggested that the person was 35 years of age, plus or minus nine years."

Based on that evidence and the information gleaned from examining other bones, Beattie was fairly confident the Trapper was more than 30 years old. "Whether he was approaching 40 years of age, I'm not sure about that," he said.

People who had seen Albert Johnson alive generally assumed from his build that he had led a physically demanding life. As a result, Beattie was surprised that he found no evidence of osteoarthritic degenerative changes.

"I would have expected that somebody of that age would have some evidence for at least the beginnings of some degenerative osteoarthritic changes in the vertebrae, and in the other joints of the skeleton, as well," he commented. "His bones didn't suggest that he had a particularly stressful lifestyle, and I think that's contradictory to what we are seeing with the story about Albert Johnson . . . That one is a bit of a head-scratcher for me."

Beattie's reading of the bones supported Andrews' findings with regard to the Mad Trapper's spine. "He had this very obvious anomaly in the lower part of his back . . . one that likely was a bit problematic for him. It could have been sore. It was likely somewhat unstable, and he may have been taking medication for it—an analgesic like the kidney pills that were found with him."

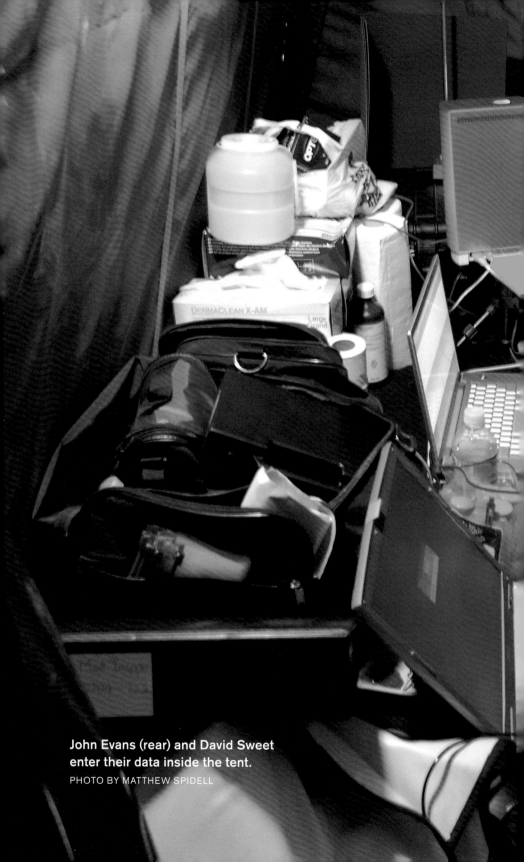

John Evans (rear) and David Sweet
enter their data inside the tent.
PHOTO BY MATTHEW SPIDELL

A finding that was not unexpected in the least was the number of bullets that had hit Albert Johnson during his final moments of life. Beattie found evidence of gunshot wounds to the leg, as well as fractured ribs on both sides of his chest that "could relate to a gunshot."

Beattie's examination also found evidence that not all of the bullets had done their damage directly. One of the anecdotes often told about the gun battle on Eagle River was that a bullet had hit the Mad Trapper in his hip, where he was carrying ammunition.[10] The 2007 exhumation supported that theory. Both Beattie and Andrews thought the spiral bone fracture and damage pattern they found when looking at the skeleton could have been caused when the ammunition was hit "with such force that it caused a piece of shrapnel to impact."

The different damage patterns made by the bullets also contributed useful information. "The keyhole entrance and exit injury to the right pelvis is important because it is of a particular shape, [which] allows the medical examiner to determine roughly the direction the shot came from," Beattie explained.

It is a known fact that in his final few minutes the Trapper was facing his pursuers, but the shape of the injury to the pelvis indicated that he had been shot from behind. "That's interesting because it looks like a catastrophic wound, [yet] it could have been one of his first gunshot injuries," Beattie noted.

The wound was critical. The Trapper was no longer physically capable of fleeing, but still he managed to continue resisting capture, dropping to the frozen river and shooting as many rounds of ammunition as he could at his pursuers. His stamina was remarkable to the end.

Like almost everyone who has looked into the details of the Mad Trapper's amazing story, Beattie was interested in uncovering more of the essence of Albert Johnson and figuring out why he'd behaved the way he had. The information Beattie gathered during the exhumation was a step toward clarifying what he calls "the mythology of the Trapper. In some respects, we do know who he was as an individual.

We know some of his physical characteristics, some of his physiological characteristics."

Although these characteristics add to the existing historical information about "the effect he had on the people during, before and after the events of the pursuit," among other things, Beattie admitted that he would be pleased if his work helped identify who the Mad Trapper really was or helped identify a living relative.

"To be able to put a first and last name on any unidentified human remains is very important. But if that doesn't happen, I don't think that's a failure. I think that we've been able to provide some kind of identity to the individual. One that provides some sense of reality, something you can touch and see and is part of history."

Beattie believes the search for more personal aspects of the Mad Trapper mystery is important to some family. "Most of us are, I think, [interested] in knowing our heritage, our history, what our connections are with the past," he explained. "If you can't put an actual name to an individual, that's a break in that chain. 'Albert Johnson' is a first and last name, but is it the *right* first and last name?

"There are people today who suspect the Trapper is a part of their family tree. It might be a good part or it might be a bad part. That's not for me to judge. There are people who would benefit from this knowledge. I think that's why it is important to make an effort to put a name to the Trapper. This individual is important in Canadian history; that's the uniqueness of him. We don't know his name—yet. We may never know his name, but if we do, then it will provide some completion of the search of some family."

Beattie is clearly hopeful that the efforts he and the other investigators have made toward identifying the Mad Trapper will lead to an eventual solution to this puzzle.

"As time goes on, techniques become more refined, they become cheaper, they become faster and they become more accurate. So what we're doing today is something that may provide the answers we need, but if they don't, maybe they just don't *yet* provide the answers that

Lynne Bell (left), Sam Andrews and Charles Furlong examine the bones, paying particular attention to the bullet hole in the pelvic bone in Owen Beattie's hand.
PHOTO BY MATTHEW SPIDELL

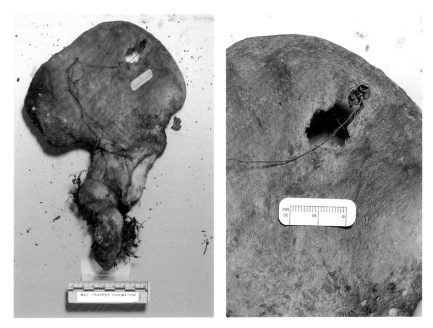

One of the bullets fired at the Trapper has left a distinct keyhole-shaped fracture in the right side of his pelvis, in an area called the ilium. PHOTOS BY MATTHEW SPIDELL

MAD TRAPPER EXHUMATION

Finding this unspent bullet in the coffin surprises everyone. PHOTO BY MATTHEW SPIDELL we need. Not being able to connect him with a living family member shouldn't be looked at as a failure. It should be looked at as something that at this time we don't yet have the capability to get the answers. There's every expectation in the future that technology will allow that answer to come forward at some stage. When? Who knows? I think it's an interim non-solution to the problem. I would look at it in an optimistic way . . . it's simply an interim attempt at a longer-term goal of fitting this person into the genealogy of some family somewhere."

Building **a Profile**

WHILE THE SKELETAL EXAMINATION CONDUCTED by Owen Beattie and Sam Andrews in the graveyard in Aklavik had confirmed a few known facts about Albert Johnson, and revealed some new ones, what we hoped might connect Albert Johnson with any potential relatives would be the results of the post-exhumation laboratory work conducted by two scientists based at universities in the Vancouver area.

Simon Fraser University's Dr. Lynne Bell is a forensic anthropologist with a special interest in tracking human movement. By examining human bones, teeth and tissue, she is able to track a person's geographic relocations through his or her lifetime. Bell used a technique known by a number of names, including bio-surveillance, geo-tracking and geo-location, to narrow a geographic area to which Aklavik's mystery man could be tied, based on an analysis of the composition of his teeth.

Bell explained that this technique evolved from archaeologists' study of paleoclimates. Scientists were already evaluating the oxygen content of rainwater and its absorption into bone and teeth to reconstruct past climates when they realized it could also be used to track movement, because the oxygen values of rainwater vary as a weather system passes across a landscape.

"If it rains, say, five times across 200 miles, the oxygen values change each time. That means geography becomes important," Bell explained. "If you can match a value to an area, then you have geo-location, and if you can match the set of [oxygen] values on one individual, then you can

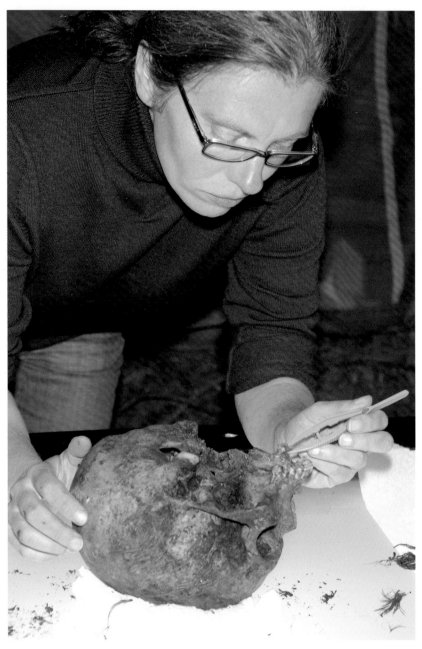

Lynne Bell examines the Mad Trapper's remaining teeth. She and her colleagues work diligently to make sure they accomplish everything they need to in the time available on site.
PHOTO BY MATTHEW SPIDELL

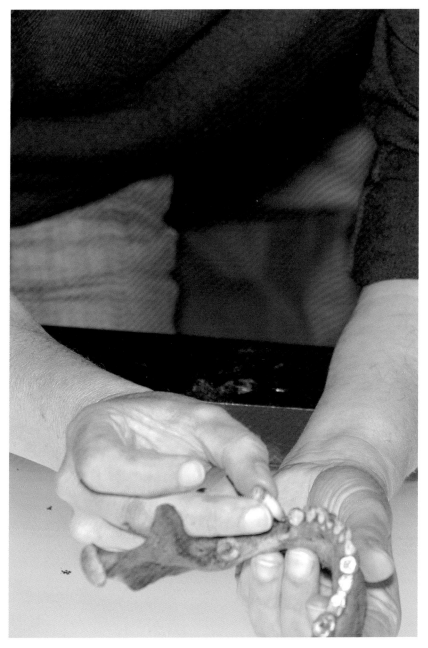

Her analysis of the Trapper's teeth will tell Bell much about where Johnson lived.

see how they've moved. We're storing a 'memory' of our environment, i.e., where we're living, in all of our tissues."

Adult teeth form in childhood, and different ones form during different periods of childhood. "Depending upon which tooth you actually sample, you're looking at a different window of years in childhood," she explained. "The enamel, the white, hard part of the tooth, is forming first, and gives us a strong childhood window into a period of years. The dentine that forms under the enamels and forms the tooth root then extends that window of time, because the dentine root actually grows longer than the crown does in terms of time. The teeth offer you a view of childhood and teenage years, so that's why they're very valuable. And once they've formed, they don't turn over. That's it. That's finished. It's kind of a time capsule of information for that individual."

In forensic work, scientists often only have a skeleton with which to work, as was the case in Aklavik. But useful information can be extracted from teeth and bones.

"[We] take small pieces of teeth and bone and subject them to chemical cleaning and then recover elemental information, isotopic information, from them."

Bell approached the Mad Trapper project with great enthusiasm despite the many unknowns about the interred body's condition. She came prepared to deal with either a fully intact human body or one that was completely skeletonized. When Albert Johnson's coffin was first opened, she saw that he *was* skeletonized—but not entirely.

"When we removed more of the soil and got a really good look at his hands and his feet and his head, it was clear that there were fingernails and toenails left."

Bell was elated. She recognized the additional information the fingernails and toenails would provide. "I had everything I needed for my type of analysis," she said, adding later how very rare and fortunate such a situation was. "I've looked at skeletal material that's 250,000 [years] to 20 years to 5 years old and have not seen fingernails. I must have looked at over 5,000 individuals in total," she remarked. "It does happen in terms of preservation, but it's rare. It was a real stroke of luck. There's something about that environment that's important, that preserved him, probably the coldness."

Once she returned from Aklavik and was back in her laboratory, Bell began her examination and analysis of the fingernail and tooth enamel samples she had recovered during the exhumation.

"I looked at the fingernails, and I took one fingernail and sub-sampled it from its most distal end—the end you would trim—right back to the nail bed. I took 10 samples. That represents approximately the last seven months of his life. It actually fits the time when [Albert Johnson] arrived in Fort McPherson until his death—it just happens to encapsulate that whole time period."

Bell examined the enamel and the root dentine. "The enamel is where I get the oxygen signature that relates to the rainwater values. It also represents a childhood [oxygen] value," she explained. "That tooth was completely formed between the ages of six to eight years, and it's telling us something about his environment—where he lived—during that period of his life. It's called a childhood signature.

"With the dentine, I'm recovering the organic portion of the collagen, and I'm getting a dietary signature from that part of his tooth. That's not necessarily helpful in geo-location, but it tells us something about his behaviour in terms of his diet, and it also gives us a window into his early life—round about 10 to 13 years of age."

Bell was especially interested in this particular data because no one knew where Albert Johnson had come from.

"It was clear to me immediately that we're not dealing with a Canadian. He did not come from Canada. His isotope value was too warm, if you like; it wasn't appropriate for what we know of Canada."

The data indicated instead that Albert Johnson might have come from the midwestern United States or a Scandinavian country. "There was some suggestion [in the past] that he could have come from Norway, and his [isotope] values fitted the Norwegian values, too. So there was a possibility that he was an American or equally possibly a European,

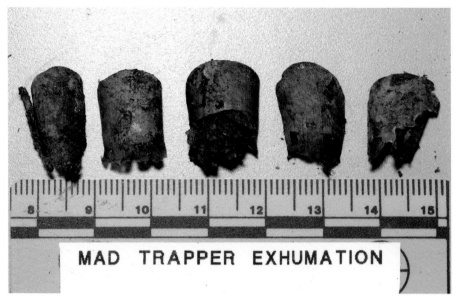

The fingernails are carefully measured, as are other remaining fragments.
PHOTO BY MATTHEW SPIDELL

but the one result from looking at his enamel is that it most likely ruled him out as being a Canadian."

That the Mad Trapper was not a Canadian surprised everyone involved with the exhumation, especially Bell. "That for me was a little unexpected, because many families had claimed him in Canada. I was half expecting a Canadian [isotope] value, perhaps not an Arctic value." But what she found "definitely set him at a real distance from Canada."

And this was not the only surprise his teeth and fingernails held.

"I had an expectation—which is a big mistake, to guess what your results are going to be—that he would show some signs of starvation in his dietary signature in his fingernail, from the period when he was on the run," she admitted. "But what I found in his fingernails was a completely different story. In terms of his nitrogen, which tells you about his protein intake, from when he arrived [in the North] he had a protein intake that I would associate with anybody living now who has a regular diet, who eats meat every day."

Weighted Annual δ¹⁸O (Delta 18 Oxygen Value)

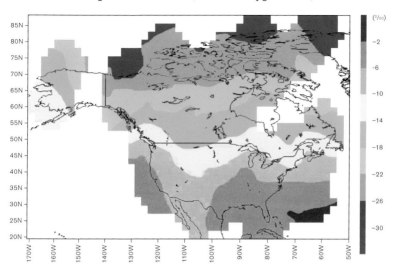

Based on samples she collects at the gravesite in Aklavik, Bell is able to analyze the oxygen levels in Albert Johnson's tooth enamel, thereby narrowing down potential regions within North America and Scandinavia. The ochre band on the top map and the yellow band on the bottom map show the latitudes within which the trace elements found in the exhumed body naturally occur. This is an annual weighted mean for precipitation values. During the course of a year, these bands move around, depending on an area's ambient temperature. As the tooth enamel sampled represents several years of formation, this is a mean for that time period. In the early stages of the investigation, this testing is valuable for ruling out other candidates. MAPS COURTESY OF THE GLOBAL NETWORK OF ISOTOPES IN PRECIPITATION PROJECT

Weighted Annual δ¹⁸O (Delta 18 Oxygen Value)

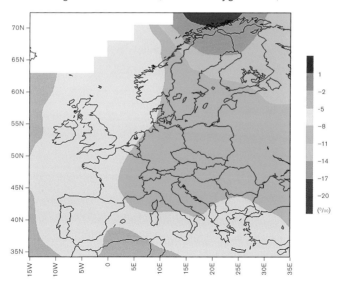

In other words, for the first months after arriving in the North from unknown whereabouts, Albert Johnson had initially eaten well. Only in the last two or three months of his life had his nitrogen signal started to drop, indicating that his diet had worsened. "It dropped significantly, so it was clear that he was getting less protein in his diet. As the winter set in, that protein intake levelled out to a much lower level."

It may not be a coincidence, then, that this was when the local police first began to receive complaints that the traplines of the First Nations residents living near Johnson were being interfered with. "The value wasn't so low as to exclude meat in his diet, but relative to what he was getting when he first arrived [in the North], it really did drop. It's intriguing, for me at any rate, that this fits with the complaints about the traps."

Bell found that "from the point when he went on the run, his protein level was at a low. It had been low prior to him going on the run, and it stayed low whilst he was on the run. And so, up to his death, his protein level remained at an all-time low."

Bell's analysis also said something about what Albert Johnson had eaten as a child. "In his childhood, he had a diet that was very similar to today's diet, in terms of people who eat meat every day in North America. There was nothing unusual in that sense from when he was in his early years—six to eight years of age—to adult life. The only big change that I saw was in the last seven months of his life, where his protein intake really changed significantly. The other aspect of the diet that came out . . . is that he appeared to have eaten a lot of maize [corn]."

However, Bell noted that some data could also indicate that Johnson had eaten a lot of marine food early in life—an interpretation that could suggest he had come from a Scandinavian country.

"If I had to make a choice about whether his isotopic values, when they're all put together, actually made him an American or a European, I think I'd have to choose American," Bell said. "He has a strong 'corn' value, and there's no real elevation in his nitrogen that is significantly high enough, I think to make him, let's say, a Norwegian or at least

Scandic. But having said that, there is the possibility that he could be European, and that can't be 100 percent ruled out, because you can get values like that if you eat marine food."

Still, Bell leans heavily toward believing Johnson was an American. "From his physiology, from the tissues I sampled, my overall feeling is that the Mad Trapper is most likely an American. It is much more likely that he was an American."

Even though she cannot pinpoint exactly where in the US the Mad Trapper came from, her results are impressive—and even more so when combined with DNA analysis.

"DNA tells us something about ancestry, and it is also a way of positively identifying someone. You can say with complete certainty that this person, in our case, Albert Johnson, is related to someone," she explained. "The isotopic data doesn't tell you anything about ancestry. It tells you about what somebody had been doing during their lifetime. It gives you life history information, behaviour.

"The two techniques [DNA and isotopic examination] fit together really well. They're very complementary. If you're dealing with somebody who's unknown—and from a forensic point of view that's a key question, because it's nearly always what we are dealing with in cold cases or skeletal material that turns up and is unknown—DNA can often be recovered. But you also need to have an idea of who the nearest family is in order to make a match.

"That's where the isotopic work comes in, particularly the oxygen work that can geo-locate. If we have some idea of where somebody was living, even in childhood, it can redirect an investigation to look at case files of missing people who would fit this individual in that time frame . . . [you] could narrow down the focus of where you're interested, and then narrow down the number of families you would potentially have to sample to make a match."

In other words, isotopic data can sometimes act as a bridge to help connect a deceased person's DNA to that of living relatives.

Having determined that the Trapper was likely from the midwestern

United States, the next logical step, if time and money were no object, would be to pinpoint a specific area.

Bell had already determined that he was from somewhere "sufficiently south for there to be corn grown in great abundance, particularly [during] this time period"—possibly the Midwest. But the question of *where* in the Midwest, an area that has a population of over 66 million people, is a question Bell was not able to answer—at least, not yet.

There are new techniques coming online all the time, she said, new technology that will allow researchers to use tiny samples and still determine a history. This should enable researchers to extrapolate information about a person's whereabouts on a month-by-month basis. "This is in the very near future," she added.

In the meantime, Bell's field is progressing at an amazing rate. "In terms of forensics, where you have to have really good accuracy to present evidence in court, for instance, we're in the early stages. We are probably at the point DNA was at in 1995. It's very much developmental right now. I think over the next 5 to 10 years we are going to see a huge amount of research in this area, to refine these geo-locating methods.

"Whilst we understand quite a lot about how this works, we haven't got enough information to uniquely and precisely locate somebody in geographical space." But even five or six years ago, scientists couldn't do what they are able to do now. In that sense, the field has already made huge strides.

Even if the area Bell had identified could be narrowed, there was the matter of connecting people from that place to the Mad Trapper. To identify any potential living relatives, someone would have to come forward and offer to have his or her DNA tested.

* * *

The scientist responsible for the DNA testing was the University of British Columbia's Dr. David Sweet, whose specialty is forensic odontology. "It is a term that describes forensic dentistry—the overlap between the dental profession on the one hand and the legal profession

Many people who had interacted with Johnson during his lifetime commented that his hair grew in tufts. Here we see that some of those tufts remain 75 years after his death.
PHOTO BY MATTHEW SPIDELL

on the other," he explained when interviewed by Michael Jorgensen. "I work with police investigators, medical examiners and coroners at crime scenes to examine dental evidence and interpret that for those investigations."

Sweet makes interpretations based on a person's unique dental traits, which include special dental fillings, distinctive anatomical patterns and various tooth characteristics.

"[It] can be a very important and scientifically based method of comparison to identify a person. This is usually one of the first methods that's used to identify the victim of crime."

Sweet was an essential member of the graveside team during the exhumation of Albert Johnson's remains, but he did not just look at the Mad Trapper's teeth.

"I was asked to play two roles when I arrived in the North and got involved with this case," he recalled. "One role was that of a dental expert, a forensic odontologist. The other was in relation to DNA evidence and trying to establish the best potential sources of DNA to try and identify this body."

Sweet had Albert Johnson's dental records from 1932, which "suggested he had some sophisticated dental treatment. As one of the first investigators, I was going to see if that dental treatment was present."

The importance of establishing this positive identification could not be overstated. "There were other indicators, like possible bullet wounds and those sorts of things, but the teeth became a very important identifier," he explained. "In forensic science it's very important to be certain of the origin of the evidence, so we did have to make sure that we were dealing with the right body. That was my role. I knew that the teeth were supposed to include some gold bridgework, some gold fillings as one example."

Armed with the detailed 1932 dental chart, Sweet became totally consumed by the project. "After some work by the others in the team, I was presented with the opportunity to see the teeth. As soon as I looked at the teeth, I could see the gold fillings. That was a very important moment for me. I've been trained to slow down, to evaluate evidence very carefully. I couldn't do it in this case. There was an excitement. My heart rate went up and I smiled. Right from the moment when I first saw those gold fillings in those specific teeth, there was a direct match to the information that we had. I knew right at that moment that we had the right person."

Sweet pointed out how unusual it was to find gold bridgework—expensive, sophisticated treatment—in a trapper. "He actually had a gold bridge to replace missing teeth and attached to the remaining teeth on each end, so we've got a sophisticated treatment that contours nicely to the dental arch and is working extremely well for him. We also have a filling that is tooth-coloured. It is a cosmetic type of filling toward the front of the mouth."

Sweet was able to determine that the cosmetically coloured filling was created at a different time than the gold filling. This finding astounded the odontologist. He was able to state emphatically, "Access to this kind of dental treatment in the Far North was non-existent. The treatments were excellent."

Sweet's reaction to what he was seeing was understandable. Finding such complex dentistry and excellent dental treatments in the mouth of a man known only as a trapper was undeniably odd.

"There was a paradox that developed in my mind about this individual who found himself in the Far North, described as a 'mad trapper,'" he explained. "[H]e must have come from what was probably a very high socioeconomic background, with—for the day—some of the best dental treatment available in the world. I can picture this man perhaps wearing a white collar and a bow tie and living in an aristocratic metropolitan area, perhaps, and yet now finding himself in the Far North. It was an unusual find, but extremely interesting, and it added to the complexity of the puzzle.

"Dental treatment like this provides a lot of clues to us. For instance, we can sometimes evaluate or estimate the amount of time that [the work] has been present in the mouth. For example, the wear on a gold

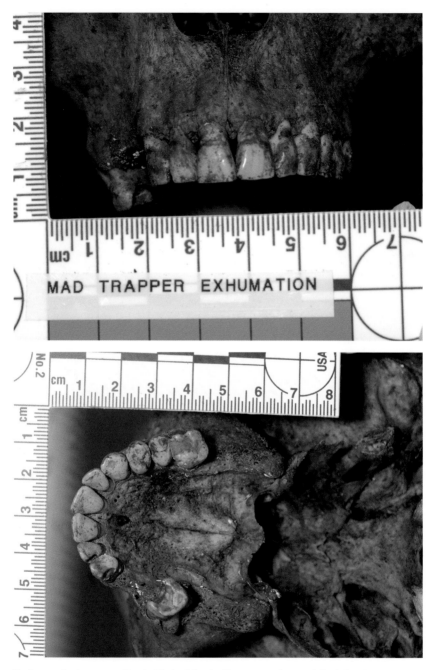

To those who know exactly what to look for, teeth can reveal a great deal about a person and the life he or she has led. PHOTOS BY MATTHEW SPIDELL

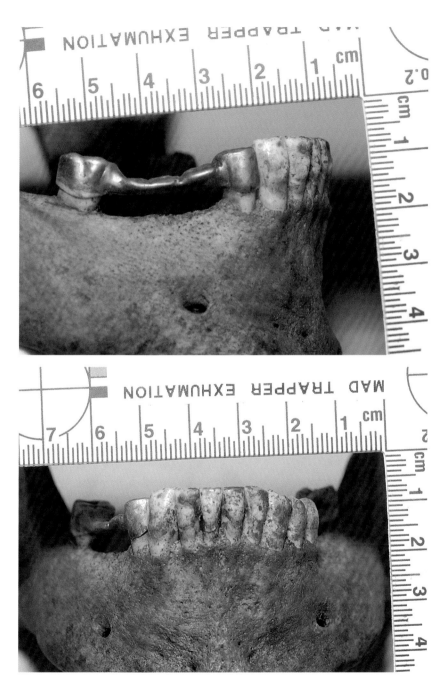

The high-quality dental work found in the Trapper's jaw suggests that at some point he had had sufficient funds to afford a good dentist. PHOTOS BY MATTHEW SPIDELL

filling or the gold bridge could tell us with a bit of certainty, at least, how long that had been there. It was my estimation that probably this gold bridge had been in place five years or longer."

Here, then, was an indication of when the man who became known as the Mad Trapper might have arrived in the Arctic.

"If you think about the alleged age of the Mad Trapper at the time of his death, it would be my sense that this filling and sophisticated dental treatment had been done in the 1920s by a very capable dentist. The [treatments] were very modern for the day. [This was] good-quality work using the latest methods. That kind of dental care usually originated in places like the northeastern United States or along the west coast of the United States in that day. Dental schools in those locations were teaching some of the most modern and up-to-date methods anywhere." So the Trapper may have been from one of these areas, he speculated.

The Mad Trapper continued to confound. "The type of words that come to mind are 'complex, enigma and paradox' when I think about the dental care in this case. This person was out of context. We would expect to see sophisticated dental treatment in someone who lived in a metropolis and was very wealthy. That wasn't the case here, obviously, so this was very, very interesting from that point of view."

Sweet was quick to refute the theory, often put forward, that the Mad Trapper had been a criminal or a gangster and had received dental treatment during periods of incarceration. "I don't think this is the kind of care that would have been available to him in an institution such as a hospital or a prison, or some institution where dentists are there just to look after the emergency needs of people. Usually inmates are helped with painful or broken teeth, and extractions may be a common thing for them to use as treatment, or maybe some straightforward fillings, but this amount of sophisticated dental care is not typical of an institutional setting."

Whoever the man calling himself Albert Johnson actually was, he clearly cared about dental hygiene—when he could. The spartan circumstances in which Johnson was living for the years prior to his death were reflected in his mouth. "There was a lot of bone loss, a lot of missing jaw structure right around the teeth. That's an indication that there was gum disease and that the problem was spreading into the bone. This absorption of the bone was causing his teeth to come loose. Teeth at the back of the mouth were missing, because they'd become loose and he'd taken them out because they weren't functioning anymore. We've got a situation where we have a person with very sophisticated dental care, but he wasn't taught or able to look after them, to keep the teeth healthy over a period of time."

Once Sweet had finished his examination of the teeth, he moved on to documenting his findings. "In a typical forensic odontology case, we actually document every aspect of the dental traits that are present in the body, so that each one of those traits can be compared to an ante-mortem dental record for the missing person," he explained. "The documentation in this case was for a different reason. We were going to rebury this individual. We needed to document through photographs, radiographs, through dental charting, as much information as we possibly could, because this would be our only opportunity."

Sweet then turned his attention to his role as a DNA expert—specifically, to the task of collecting DNA evidence.

"We wanted to collect samples from the body that were the best possible sources of DNA evidence. In this case, we chose samples from teeth," he explained. "We took samples from both the upper and lower jaw, and we also took a sample from one of the leg bones, because that is one of the blood-producing sites in life. It is very high-producing, metabolically active, and therefore is an excellent source of DNA evidence."

Once again the cold climate in which the corpse had been buried proved helpful. Sweet was pleasantly surprised to be able to collect DNA from the marrow that was preserved inside the leg bone. "We recovered a sample from the bone that was several centimetres long," he commented. "It was a large sample . . . we wanted to make sure we had a sufficient amount for our first DNA analysis. We found a full result right away, and didn't have to revisit the rest of the sample."

Back at his lab, the sample taken from "the original parent exhibit was ground into a powder using a sample-processing technique that we've developed at my lab, using liquid nitrogen," Sweet explained. "The nitrogen keeps the sample very cool, makes it brittle, so it will be pulverized in a way that will maximize the amount of DNA in the sample. The liquid nitrogen is placed in a freezer mill. The tooth is ground with a plunger that goes back and forth inside of a tube, and the resulting powder is able to be treated with chemical scissors, which opens up the cells and allows the DNA to come out in a solution. We're looking for different lengths of DNA. That's what forensic scientists use to compare one person to another."

As is standard in his field, Sweet then confirmed his results with additional testing "to be sure that (a) the DNA result only came from the body of the Mad Trapper and (b) that the initial result was confirmed, verified, as being accurate, that it was reproducible. For these tests both tooth and bone were used."

Although the techniques the forensic odontologist used to create a DNA profile for Albert Johnson were routine, the results he obtained were not. "In my role as a DNA expert, and in working with DNA from teeth and other types of tissue in the human body, I've looked at very old remains," he explained. "I've looked at 900-year-old cases, and even at cases that are 50 years old, where we never get a DNA result. I was very surprised when we got a full DNA profile. I was elated. I don't know how to interpret that result. It's another part of the enigma—a paradox. We've got a situation where we can't get DNA sometimes in cases that are only two years old, and here we get a full DNA result from someone who's been in the ground for 75 years. I believe that the permafrost may have had something to do with it. It preserved the evidence very well."

Once Sweet had successfully created the profile of the Mad Trapper's unique DNA sequences, which he would then compare to those of potential relatives to see if there was a match, he was ready to receive blood samples from families whose histories seemed to indicate that they might have been related to the man gunned down on Eagle River on that frigid February day in 1932.

Sweet's perspective on the man who was the Mad Trapper had changed considerably in the months since the dig. "I've come to know the Mad Trapper not as a madman. He was certainly a recluse, and the type of person who was trying to elude something in his past, but he comes from a high level of class in his society originally. He had some wealth and he had an interest in his personal health, in the sense he was able to seek out and obtain some of the most sophisticated treatment of the day. He was able to afford it and he was able to know the importance of it, so he had a sophistication about himself that is portrayed in the evidence that we have. But, he is also someone who could survive in the wilderness in very harsh conditions and evade capture from people who were trained. He's a wonderful study in human nature, and we can only speculate in terms of where he got those abilities and capacities to survive."

*   *   *

After the exhumation, John Evans put us in touch with Glenn Woods, a psychological profiler he thought might be able to reveal more of the essence of the man known as the Mad Trapper.

In May 2007, Glenn Woods retired as director of behavioural sciences after a 35-year career with the RCMP, but he continues to work independently in the field. He also chairs the education committee of the International Criminal Investigative Analysis Fellowship (ICIAF). The ICIAF is a professional association whose members—generally police and academics—have undertaken training as psychological or geographical profilers and have met specific, demanding criteria. Training to be a psychological profiler like Woods takes place over a period of two to three years, during which candidates attend university courses in psychology and psychiatry, among other disciplines, and complete understudy sessions with three different police departments.

Woods served his first two practicums with the Ontario Provincial Police and the New York City Police before serving the standard final session with the FBI, the organization that created and defined this particular field of expertise. Once he'd met all of these criteria, he had to pass a rigorous exam. Meeting all of these qualifications requires "quite a commitment," Woods explained.

While he was eminently qualified to produce a psychological profile of Albert Johnson, Woods was initially unfamiliar with the story of the Mad Trapper. We supplied him with background material that we thought would prove useful. We hoped it would enable him to reveal the psychological makeup of the elusive man, to tell us the essence of the man whose efforts to avoid capture had mesmerized the world in 1932.

Once Woods had familiarized himself with the legend of the Mad Trapper, he was ready to share his thoughts with Michael Jorgensen.

To establish context for his analysis, Woods first explained that everyone has "a baseline for impulse-coping mechanisms." For instance, under normal circumstances a law-abiding person going to work in the morning would drive in a manner that is safe and considerate of other drivers, resisting any impulse to drive erratically. But if the same person has had an argument with her spouse, or perhaps is hungover from a late-night party the previous evening, such extenuating factors could alter her baseline of impulse control, resulting in her speeding or running a red light.

Or, in the case of a robbery where a store clerk has been killed, the baseline for impulse control might indicate that the thief has robbed various corner stores over the years but never harmed anyone. "What changed?" Woods asked rhetorically. "It could be that this particular store clerk remind[ed] the robber of his father—whom he hated." In other words, one variable can be the trigger that changes a thief's usual behaviour from robbery to murder.

Woods explained that in modern policing, when authorities are aware of a person in the community who has the potential to be dangerous, they keep the information they have about that person as current

His expertise as a behavioural scientist allows Glenn Woods to provide insight into Johnson's personality and possible motivations.
PHOTO COURTESY OF GLENN WOODS

as possible. The police need to know if anything changes in the person's life that might alter his or her baseline of impulse control and therefore make the individual more of a threat.

Of course, the authorities in the Northwest Territories during the early 1930s did not have the luxury of threat-assessment updates. They knew only that Albert Johnson was a loner who avoided interactions with other people. Woods, however, was able to read considerably more into that loner's behaviour.

"The Trapper was an anal, meticulous guy. He was a man who liked to be outside, to be free, away from people," Woods explained. "The police coming to the door could have been seen by the Trapper as jeopardizing that freedom. Constable King's knock on that cabin door must have seemed like an explosion of unwanted noise to Albert Johnson.

"He might have felt cornered. In his mind, he needed to prevent anyone from coming into his cabin. He was certainly running from something, [and] the threat of going to jail would have been extremely serious for a man with his personality. That alone could have been the catalyst that set the tragic events in motion."

Woods had other insights to share. "[Albert Johnson] was neither a thief nor a rounder. Whatever he was running from was important enough for him to cut himself off from his past. He may have committed some criminal act. He was disciplined and principled; therefore, either some principle or mental flaw caused him to act out and do things that showed bad judgement."

Woods' analysis supported my long-held disagreement with the premise that the Mad Trapper had been a career criminal before seeking asylum in the anonymity of the Arctic—even more strongly than had the sophisticated dental work found in his mouth.

His analysis also supported the theory that there are different types of criminals. In the world of psychological profilers, Woods explained, criminals generally fall into one of two categories: howlers or hunters.

"A howler will threaten over and over again that the police had better leave him alone or he'll shoot. Then if the police don't leave he may shoot, but only a harmless warning shot.

"[Albert Johnson] was not into warning. He was a hunter. He offered no warning, [but] just fired an offensive shot. Shooting through the door at [RCMP Constable] King was cold. It was a desperate act by a desperate man."

Woods also noted that Johnson's actions gave every indication that he was a smart and decisive person. So why did he not flee from his cabin after shooting Constable King? After all, he must have known the police would come back.

No one, not even an expert, can know what was going on in Johnson's head. But, as Woods pointed out, "Even good decision-makers can procrastinate . . . and smart people make bad decisions when they're otherwise focussed."

If there is one single quality that defined Johnson's personality for Woods, it was that the man was not afraid of death. But he was not suicidal.

"It would have been a contradiction of his personality," Woods explained. "Albert Johnson knew that he had to do what he had to do, and that if he died doing that, then his death was simply inevitable. When the police came to his door, he was probably not thinking through to the consequences of his actions. Things snowballed as a result of that, and he created a situation that he had to deal with. He likely understood that death was the probable outcome of the events. The Trapper seemed to lack emotion."

Woods stressed that Johnson's way of thinking was "practical, not fantasy-based." So what does that say about the confusing tracks the fugitive cleverly created for his pursuers to follow? Was he mocking or taunting the police? There are many modern-day examples of criminals who contact the police and taunt them about how clever they are, bragging that the authorities will never catch them. "To the bad guy, the taunting can become the most important aspect of the crime," Woods pointed out.

He thinks there could have been an element of taunting involved when Albert Johnson designed circular paths for the police to follow, but then again, those actions were also an effective way to elude his potential captors. Given the severity of the weather conditions, the more time the searchers wasted going in futile circles, the greater the likelihood that they would be unwilling or unable to continue.

In any case, the Trapper's actions remained overwhelmingly practical. Woods believed he wanted to escape. "His actions were extremely decisive. He knew how to survive—to an almost superhuman skill level."

But while he was a skilled survivalist, the Mad Trapper was also a loner—an aspect of his personality that Woods took time to analyze. "Johnson was antisocial—a hermit," he concluded. "Antisocial people don't have a lot of attachments. A true hermit is very unusual, because

This 1930 photograph shows how remote the hamlet of
Aklavik is when the final posse sets out after the Mad Trapper.
Seventy-five years later, the area is just as isolated.

human beings like interaction. But Albert Johnson was very happy being alone. He enjoyed his own company. People who were near him [before the chase] reported hearing him singing, humming and whistling. He liked being alone."

In fact, Johnson's desire to be alone may be what kicked off the seven-week manhunt that led to his death. "He did not want to be interfered with," explained Woods. "Constable King and Johnson were a dichotomy: King just wanted a simple interaction with Johnson, [whereas] Johnson wanted no interaction with anyone."

In light of Woods' conclusion that the Mad Trapper had no interest in anyone else, it is ironic that even after 75 years, there are people so interested in him that they are willing to go to tremendous trouble and expense to find out anything they can about him—and even try to prove a relationship with him.

And we would not be leaving Albert Johnson alone any time soon, because, armed with the DNA profile created by Dr. Sweet, we finally had the chance to verify his potential relatives' claims, and in so doing perhaps reveal a little more about the mysterious Mad Trapper.

A FACIAL RECONSTRUCTION

During the exhumation, John Evans measured Albert Johnson's skull and passed along that data to facial-reconstruction artist Andrea Stevenson Won so she could generate a picture of what the Mad Trapper might have looked like at the time of his death.

An amalgamation of artistry, forensic science, anthropology, osteology and anatomy, forensic facial reconstruction is easily the most subjective technique in the field of forensic anthropology. Based on skull measurements, the position and general shape of the main facial features will be mostly accurate, but subtle identifying features like wrinkles, birthmarks, skin folds and the shapes of the nose and ears can only be approximated, since skeletal remains leave no evidence of these aspects of a person's appearance.

Even so, an image such as the one shown here can be useful when all other identification techniques have failed, because someone may recognize the individual pictured.

Looking for **a Match**

WHILE DR. SWEET WAS PREPARING the DNA profile, Dr. Bell was creating her isotope analyses and the production crew was processing hours of film, Carrie Gour faced what was perhaps the most daunting task of all—handling the media inquiries that followed the exhumation.

Even though the public had been excluded from the dig, people knew it was taking place and were curious about it. Gour's phone rang almost nonstop for the rest of August 2007. Newspaper and magazine journalists as well as radio and television reporters from coast to coast wanted to know all about the project.

Once their stories had been printed and aired, the deluge of interest and inquiries from the public accelerated and did not stop for weeks. It seemed that news of Myth Merchant's project had reached even the most isolated areas of the continent. Queries from people who thought they might be related to Albert Johnson came in by phone, mail and email. One of the administrative duties I took on was replying to the hundreds of inquiries.

Not everyone who contacted us felt they had a genetic connection to Johnson. As a matter of fact, the only common ground among those who wrote or phoned was a deep emotional interest in the mystery— and, for some, a desire to help solve it.

Several people were sure the police had chased not Albert Johnson, but another trapper who happened to be visiting Johnson's cabin during the winter of 1931–32. Others had dramatic stories to relate, but nothing that could be verified by DNA—which, of course, was the point of our exercise. (One man prefaced his input with the refreshingly honest comment, "This is probably highly unreliable, but . . . " It was good to get the warning.)

A few folks went to a great deal of trouble to get tiny scraps of information to us when they suspected they were tidbits we did not have—and then wished us well on our quest. Others were clearly offended by our project and were vehement in their opinions that we should immediately call a halt to the identification process and let the dead rest in peace. (One person who took great offence at the exhumation had clearly confused the Mad Trapper with the famous Grey Owl.) And some people wanted to express their displeasure with the use of "the pejorative term 'Mad Trapper.'"

While we were glad to hear from everyone, we were most excited by the letters from people who thought they might be close enough relations of the Mad Trapper for us to consider them for DNA testing.

Before proceeding to the expensive DNA testing, I needed to collect as much family history about the candidates as I could, so we could confirm that the facts people presented agreed with what we knew about Albert Johnson—that their genealogy led back to one of the areas of the world identified by Dr. Bell's isotope work and included a male ancestor who had gone missing during the mid- to late 1920s, one who was at least approximately the same height, weight and age of the man known as the Mad Trapper. Much to some people's disappointment, I could only recommend testing the families whose DNA profiles matched these benchmarks.

It became clear that a great many families have their own myths and secrets, and that these stories can be extremely convoluted. Some people who phoned or wrote in requested total confidentiality, for fear of embarrassing younger family members, while others wanted the matter aired in order to clear up family conflicts.

One man was so sure of his direct connection to Albert Johnson that he was anxious to tell his story to the national press. An elderly woman who grew up wondering whether the Trapper was her uncle apparently could not bring herself to contact us directly, so had a psychologist of her acquaintance act as her representative.

Of course, no portion of the Mad Trapper story would be complete without some confusion. A few correspondents were sure that the name "Albert Johnson" was an alias chosen by their supposed relative, while people whose missing ancestor actually was named Albert Johnson were equally sure it *was* his real name.

One woman wrote to tell us her grandfather had once owned a lumberyard in a small Ontario town. He had disappeared with the company's payroll and been last seen on a train. That was all the information she could give us, but the timelines did fit the Trapper story. She hoped her letter would lead to the solution of two mysteries—her family's and that of Albert Johnson's true identity.

Some people sent copies of wonderful old family photographs to demonstrate why they had always thought the Mad Trapper was their great-uncle, the relative most commonly suggested. Odds that the man killed on February 17, 1932, on the Eagle River had had children were probably slim, but it seemed possible that he might have been someone's great-uncle.

After we examined people's stories to be sure the ancestor they thought might have been Albert Johnson had come from an area identified by Dr. Bell's mapping research and been born in the late 1890s, we asked for any known physical attributes. Did they know how tall their relative had been, or whether he spoke English with any sort of a discernible accent? Were there any family stories that had been passed down through the generations that might contain useful information for us? Many people responded with heartwarming generosity, while others were so confident that they came across with decidedly pompous attitudes.

The first DNA sample we requested was from a Kamloops man whose father had deserted his family in the mid- to late 1920s. This person's circumstantial evidence—approximate age, physical stature and time of disappearance—lined up so well that everyone involved in the identification project was hopeful of a match.

I mailed the man's DNA sample to Sweet's testing facility at the University of British Columbia, a 20-minute flight or a 1.5-hour ferry ride from my home on Vancouver Island. We were eager to test the sample as soon as possible, but it took nearly two weeks for the precious envelope to make the journey via regular mail. (When he finally did get it, Sweet spoke for all of us when he said, "We can exhale now.")

To our great disappointment, the DNA testing revealed that the man's father could not have been the Mad Trapper. However, the experience *did* teach us to use faster methods of delivering samples in the future.

In the meantime, the publicity continued to attract interest and bring inquiries from coast to coast.

Author Dick North had been convinced for years that "Albert Johnson" was an alias used by Johnny Johnson, a petty criminal from North Dakota. In the course of his research, North had been in contact with Yukon resident Ole Getz, a trapper and log-home builder who had been raised in Norway.

Trapper and log-home builder Ole Getz grew up in Norway listening to exciting tales about his relatives who had immigrated to North America.
PHOTO BY MICHAEL JORGENSEN

Getz's boyhood had been rich with exciting stories about the adventures of his mother's uncle, Johnny Johnson, who had immigrated to North America in the early part of the 20th century and made his fortune in gold and furs.

In reality, it turned out that this uncle's family had settled in North Dakota and were barely scraping by. As a young man, Johnny had turned to petty crime to support himself. By the 1920s, Johnny Johnson's relatives back in Norway had lost track of him, and simply presumed he had died of natural causes. The possibility that he had instead become the infamous Mad Trapper, as Dick North was suggesting, was a revelation to the family. Based on that possibility, Getz contacted Myth Merchant Films and asked to be included in the DNA-testing process.

Despite the Getz family's belief that they were related to the Mad Trapper, a large shadow shrouded the likelihood that the man gunned down on the Eagle River and Ole Getz's great uncle were one and the same. Johnny Johnson, it seemed, had lived his entire life in poverty. If he had ever seen a dentist, it would have been in one of the handful of prisons where he was incarcerated during the 1920s. It was highly improbable that anyone with his background could have received anything more than the most rudimentary dental care—certainly nothing approaching Albert Johnson's sophisticated dental work. Still, every angle of every lead had to be pursued until it could be ruled out entirely, so as soon as Getz supplied the drop of blood for DNA testing, we rushed the specimen to the lab.

Coincidentally, another strong candidate came to our attention the same week we were in contact with Ole Getz. Ontario resident Suzanne Young and her sisters had recently unravelled a long and convoluted family tale—one that seemed to lead directly to the Mad Trapper. Family photos showed an uncanny physical resemblance between their grandmother and Albert Johnson. We certainly agreed that the two could have been brother and sister, as Young wondered. In addition, her great-uncle had disappeared shortly before Johnson

WAS YOUR GREAT-UNCLE THE MAD TRAPPER?

To evaluate the likelihood that a particular person had been the Mad Trapper, we compared the description about him provided by the potential relative with what we knew about the Mad Trapper from first-hand observations, the original autopsy report and new information obtained through the exhumation and subsequent laboratory analyses. How closely the description matched the following benchmarks determined whether the relative's DNA would be tested.

ALBERT JOHNSON

Sex: Male.

Race: White.

Born: Late 1890s.

Died: February 17, 1932 (in his mid-30s at time of death).

Height: Average (estimated as being 5 feet 9 inches).

Weight: 170 pounds in the summer of 1931, and 140 pounds at death (estimates).

Hair: Light brown (frequently described as growing in "tufts").

Eyes: Blue.

Remarks: Arrived in Fort McPherson, Northwest Territories, in July 1931; may have been born or lived in Midwestern United States or Scandinavia; reclusive by nature; skilled survivalist and marksman; spoke English with a Scandinavian accent; well-proportioned, stocky build and noticeably stooped posture (suffered from scoliosis, for which he may have taken pain pills); sophisticated dental work dating from the 1920s found in his mouth (including tooth-coloured and gold fillings and a gold bridge), plus five pieces of gold dental work in his possession at time of death (likely removed from his own mouth because gum disease was spreading into his jawbone and causing teeth to come loose); carrying small glass bottles containing five pearls and a sizeable quantity of alluvial gold.

appeared in the North and would have been approximately the same age.

Much to our disappointment, the initial DNA tests did not *entirely* support either Ole Getz or Sue Young as being descendents of the Mad Trapper. Because the results were not absolutely conclusive, the blood samples from those candidates needed to be sent for an additional round of testing. This second round proved to be both time-consuming and expensive, but we had no choice other than to proceed with it.

Several weeks later, the results were in: neither Young nor Getz was related to the Mad Trapper. In Getz's case, it was a double disappointment, because it also meant the man killed on the Eagle River in February of 1932 was not his great-uncle, Johnny Johnson, thus disproving Dick North's theory.

By early summer of 2008, the likeliest descendents had been ruled out. We needed to regroup and reassess who were the strongest remaining candidates and test their DNA. Without too much hope, we requested and submitted another six samples to Dr. Sweet's laboratory.

In the meantime, Gour and Jorgensen had been in contact with a man living in Alberta named Mark Fremmerlid, who—like Ole Getz—had grown up with tales of his great-uncle.

Sigvald Haaskjold was a young man in the early 1900s when he left the family's Norwegian homestead to travel to Canada. His family lost track of him, but never ceased to wonder what had become of him, although they had never made any connection between him and the Mad Trapper.

When Fremmerlid was a young adult, a casual conversation that wound its way around to the topic of family histories caused him to connect the two pieces of history. Initially, the connection seemed tenuous, but it set Fremmerlid on a mission to prove that his great-uncle had renamed himself Albert Johnson and was, in fact, the Mad Trapper. Through extensive research, Fremmerlid had strong circumstantial evidence, and the book he wrote and self-published in 2007[11] made a convincing case.

It was a claim we could not ignore. Haaskjold was from a portion of Norway identified through Bell's isotope work as Albert Johnson's homeland. Further, he had a living relative who was a generation older than he, and who was willing to provide a DNA sample (increasing the accuracy of the DNA testing). He had pursued his investigation as far as he could without access to DNA comparison and had not run into any contradictory indications. But the anomaly of the sophisticated dental work remained. Fremmerlid's ancestor had come to Canada to earn money so as not to lose the family's farm in Norway. It was difficult to imagine that a family in such dire straits would have been able to afford the expensive dentistry found in the Trapper's skull, but we had no way to disprove this possibility.

I anxiously began corresponding with Fremmerlid's aunt in Norway. As soon as I had the DNA samples from both nephew and aunt, I couriered them to Dr. Sweet's lab and we began the now-familiar process of waiting.

Within a few days the results were in: neither of Fremmerlid's relatives was a match, nor were any of the remaining candidates.

It was the end of July 2008, almost a year after the exhumation of the Mad Trapper's remains, and we still had no answer to the question that had driven this long, sometimes tedious and always expensive investigation. We had vetted hundreds of inquiries, calmed a handful of folks and corrected many others in their misconceptions about Albert Johnson. We had reviewed dozens of family histories and selected candidates for DNA testing who met the criteria we had established.

After the initial disappointment with our first candidate, we had all reined in our optimism. Even so, each blood sample sent to Sweet's laboratory was accompanied by the great hopes of many people. And each time the lab determined that the submission was not a match, our hopes were dashed. This process repeated itself a dozen more times, until we finally ran out of qualified candidates for testing.

What to do? Deadlines were approaching. Discovery Channel was anxious to have the completed documentary, and those who had submitted DNA for testing were eager to know whether they were related to Albert Johnson. At this point, only the scientists, the filmmakers and I knew that we had so far been unsuccessful in finding anyone related to the Mad Trapper. Everyone else, including potential relatives who had submitted their DNA for testing, had to wait until the documentary aired on the Discovery Channel in 2009. The whole world, it seemed, was waiting to see whether we had succeeded in identifying the Mad Trapper.

All of a sudden, 10 months after the DNA-testing process had begun and within a matter of days of each other, two families from different parts of northern Ontario contacted us. In both cases, the anecdotal evidence was strong: the birth date and disappearance date of the missing ancestor conformed to what we knew about Albert Johnson.

These families' histories were especially intriguing to Sweet, who had developed a personal interest in uncovering the identity of Albert Johnson. He admitted that he "really had to take off [his] forensic hat" at times, lest he get caught up with what might turn out to be no more than a family legend.

"As a forensic scientist going into a normal case, we try to avoid coming to any conclusion based on the circumstantial evidence," he said. "We want to just go with the scientific conclusions. It shouldn't matter to me, as a forensic scientist, the strength of the suspected family members' ties to the Mad Trapper, but I was quite excited to be able to compare these, because I thought that we would be able to come up with identification."

We quickly replenished our supplies of DNA-testing kits and sent one out to each of these newest applicants. Again we waited.

And again, neither sample was a match. We were no closer to determining the Mad Trapper's true identity than we had been mere days after the dig in August 2007.

But as disappointed as we were, we were also tremendously satisfied to have taken the puzzle further than anyone else ever had and, in doing so, revealed information that had been previously unknown. And there was the distinct possibility that this information might prove useful in the future. At least, Dr. Sweet thought so.

"In typical forensic science cases, when we have an exclusion, and we don't have a linkage for a particular person, investigators continue to search for more information that can lead them to possible sources that would be better than the cases that have already been compared. I think that's the next step in this case. For additional family members that think they're related to the Mad Trapper to step forward.

"Somebody out there is related in his family tree, and we just haven't found them yet. We have the technology. We have the evidence from the Trapper's body to be able to compare to those suspected family members, so the next step is to find the family member who is related and then to show that relationship.

"Some people might think it's very difficult to continue this because we're so far down the line [generationally] now. We have a situation where we've collected DNA evidence, but how are we going to find the family member so distant from this person and make comparisons? The fact is we do have the technology. The science is there to be able to help us to do that. It's the human factor that's going to be the limiting factor . . . finding the right family member."

Despite Sweet's confidence that a match can be made in the future, Myth Merchant Films will not be involved in any further DNA testing. Satisfied that they have pursued every avenue available under the circumstances, Michael Jorgensen and Carrie Gour consider their team's attempt to identify the Mad Trapper finished.

But if a person armed with the new information revealed by this project should make their own testing arrangements, who knows? The two television producers just might be willing to make a sequel to *Hunt for the Mad Trapper*.

Conclusion

It's an interesting coincidence of timing that I am writing these words today, almost exactly one year after the body of the Mad Trapper was exhumed. During the intervening 12 months, we have used every tool available to us—from basic archival research and tried-and-true interpersonal communication to cutting-edge forensics research techniques—to learn what we can about the Mad Trapper. The results of all these investigations have not only added previously unknown facts to Albert Johnson's case file, but have also dispelled some long-held myths about the Mad Trapper.

From an analysis of the dental work found in Johnson's mouth, we now know that his background was not one of poverty. If he didn't live in a large metropolitan area where such sophisticated dentistry was available, he at least had access to such a centre. The dental work also implies that he had enough knowledge—education, perhaps—to appreciate its importance.

We also know that the man's stooped posture—always assumed to have been the result of a life of hard, physical labour—was actually caused by scoliosis, a spinal deformity.

The theory that Albert Johnson was a criminal has been emphatically ruled out, as has the possibility that he was born or raised in Canada. It is likely he came from the corn belt of the United States, or possibly a Scandinavian country. The fact that he survived for seven weeks while running from the RCMP indicates that he was extremely well versed in survival techniques, which he likely acquired during military training.

While we know these things about Albert Johnson, we still don't have the definitive answer about his identity. It seems that the enigma who led authorities on an almost superhuman chase through some of the harshest conditions this planet can create has once again succeeded in eluding his pursuers.

But that may not always be the case. Albert Johnson arrived in the North just as the Great Depression was beginning. Countless hundreds of men who may have been working hard to barely support their families were suddenly unable to find work. Many of those men simply walked away and, for all intents and purposes, disappeared—at a time when there were still first-hand accounts of miners making fabulous finds in the gold rush. Viewed from that perspective, is it any wonder that we found so many families with stories that seemed to fit with the tale of the Mad Trapper?

Today, of course, with the paper trails we all create in our everyday lives, it would be almost impossible to disappear in this way. But we must remember that at the time of the Mad Trapper—as the histories of the families who contacted us attest—vanishing was not just possible, but, sadly, fairly common. It is ironic that while these family stories of missing men have no ending, we know how the story of Albert Johnson ends, but not how it began.

Real-life mysteries are just not that easy to solve. No matter how many experts you involve, you are not necessarily going to arrive at conclusive or even satisfying results—and certainly not within an hour, as we are all so accustomed to seeing on television dramas about forensic examiners.

"Nobody knew who he was when he arrived [in the Arctic], and even with all this effort and forensic research, we still don't know who he was," Bell said. "He's one step ahead of us in terms of keeping his identity from us. We've done everything we can do in terms of forensic techniques, in terms of new techniques, developmental techniques. The expertise that was brought to this case, and all the historical research that went on—

I mean, it was a huge undertaking. And yet we still haven't solved it. We still don't know who this guy is. So he's kind of laughing at us, I think."

Of course, it is considerably easier for Dr. Bell and the other forensic experts involved in the Mad Trapper project to accept inconclusive results than it is for the general public. Inherent in scientific investigation is an understanding that any carefully executed and documented work is of vital importance because, at the very least, it provides a base for future researchers to build upon. While a particular experiment or project might only contribute to solving a problem by determining what is *not* the answer, the work undertaken still saves future researchers from having to spend time and resources probing the same ground.

Even so, the scientists involved with the project were not immune to feeling frustrated that Johnson's true identity remains unknown. "In the end, I have mixed emotions," Sweet admitted. "I'm really disappointed in one way that we weren't able to solve the puzzle. Scientists have an arrogance about being able to throw all of the modern technology and the modern methods they have at their disposal at trace evidence, and come up with an answer. But it's a forensic reality that some cases remain unsolved."

But the case of the Mad Trapper may one day be solved. There may be families out there who had never considered the possibility of being related to Albert Johnson, because the usual descriptions of him simply did not fit with their genealogies. Because the DNA of possible relations can now be tested and compared to the Mad Trapper's, there may one day be a match that will reveal our mystery man's identity.

In the meantime, I have learned a great deal more about a character who has fascinated me for years, and I am secretly pleased by the fact that Albert Johnson—whoever he may have been—has succeeded in protecting his secrets for more than 75 years.

Endnotes

1   Constable William Carter's 1932 report, Library and Archives Canada. It is unfortunate that the RCMP had not been aware—if it was indeed true—that Johnson had aimed a gun at the Aboriginal trappers who had allegedly paid him a visit. Had they been, it is unlikely they would have sent such a small and vulnerable party to follow up on the complaints about Johnson.

2   In a 1938 magazine article, Albert Johnson was called the "Fiend of Rat River." In many ways that moniker is more accurate than the "Mad Trapper of Rat River," because his only association with trapping were the accusations of the Aboriginal trappers and his actions, which proved he was cunning, but not necessarily mad.

3   This description of the cabin's demolition is the version most commonly told; in his 1932 report, however, Constable William Carter quotes Inspector Eames as reflecting that "the dynamite did practically no damage to the cabin, and it wasn't until after Johnson had [later] escaped [that] the cabin was destroyed by manual labour, so that Johnson could not return and again use it as a so-called fort."

4   Constable William Carter's 1932 report, Library and Archives Canada.

5   At the height of the Arctic manhunt, an estimated 30 men and 133 dogs were involved in the search for Johnson. One of those men, clearly a master of the understatement, made this comment about the weather conditions and his reaction to them: "At -50°F, I was damn chilly."

6 If the hunt had not ended when it did, the authorities would have been up against a serious shortage of ammunition.

7 In the first days of Sergeant Hersey's hospitalization, he complained of discomfort from what he thought was a crease in his bed sheets. When Dr. Urquhart investigated his patient's complaint, he discovered that considerably more than a wrinkled sheet was causing the problem. After Urquhart surgically removed the bullet lodged in the sergeant's back, Hersey was much more comfortable and he had a unique souvenir from the shootout that had nearly cost him his life.

8 Although it looked insignificant once it was finally exposed in August 2007, Johnson's original coffin measured just over 6 feet by 3 feet. The man who built it had never made such a thing before, nor did he ever do it again. His son told Michael Jorgensen that he still remembers having heard bones break as the frozen body was jammed into the plain wooden box.

9 Someone observed that the Mad Trapper mystery was the ultimate cold case, but it was a cold case with a twist, because we know who killed the subject of the investigation; what we don't know is who that subject was.

10 In his 1932 report, Constable William Carter noted, "Johnson carried a box of .22 ammunition in his hip pocket. It was later determined that someone had hit the ammunition with a . . . bullet making quite a mess of the hip."

11 Fremmerlid's self-published book is called *What Became of Sigvald, Anyway? Was He the Mad Trapper of Rat River?*

Select Bibliography

Books

Anderson, F.W., and Art Downs. *The Death of Albert Johnson, Mad Trapper of Rat River.* Surrey, BC: Heritage House, 1986.

Fremmerlid, Mark. *What Became of Sigvald Anyway? Was He The Mad Trapper of Rat River?* [n.p.]: Self-published, 2007.

Katz, Hélèna. *The Mad Trapper: The Incredible Tale of a Famous Canadian Manhunt.* Canmore, AB: Altitude Publishing, 2004.

Koehler, Steven A., and Cyril H. Wecht. *Postmortem: Establishing The Cause of Death.* Richmond Hill, ON: Firefly Books, 2006.

Lyle, D.P. *Forensics For Dummies.* Hoboken, NJ: Wiley Publishing Inc., 2004.

North, Dick. *The Mad Trapper of Rat River: A True Story of Canada's Biggest Manhunt.* Toronto: Macmillan of Canada, c. 1972.

Periodicals

The Quarterly (Spring and Winter 1998). Royal Canadian Mounted Police.

The day after the dig, before the team members went their separate ways, a willing passerby snapped this photo of the group at Inuvik's Mike Zubko Airport. Front row (left to right): Igal Petel, Sean Feldstein, Michael Carroll, Al Lead, Gary Rutherford, Brent Gilbert. Back row (left to right): Matthew Spidell, Sam Andrews, Lynne Bell, Owen Beattie, Barbara Smith, John Evans, Carrie Gour, Mel Benson, David Sweet, Michael Jorgensen.

ACKNOWLEDGEMENTS

To Michael Jorgensen and Carrie Gour of Myth Merchant Films—
thank you for inviting me to be a part of this adventure. Thank you to the
people of Aklavik, Northwest Territories—your gracious hospitality was
deeply appreciated. To Mr. Dennis Allen, Dr. Sam Andrews, Dr. Owen
Beattie, Dr. Lynne Bell, Mr. John Evans, Dr. David Sweet and Mr. Glenn
Woods—thank you all for your kindness and patience in dealing with my
(perhaps seemingly) endless inquiries. Warm thanks to Andrea Stevenson
Won of Biomodal for sharing the facial reconstruction she created, to
Shirlee Bucknall for her technical assistance with the oxygen maps,
1932 coroner's report and Ole Getz photo, and to the staff at the RCMP
Museum for their cooperation and help.

Usually, I have to thank my friends and family for their patience in
listening to me talk non-stop about a book for the period of time in which
I was researching and writing it. With this book, I must say thank you to
those same folks for understanding that I couldn't say anything at all
about the project. Finally you can "read all about it."

My biggest debt of gratitude, though, goes to my husband, Bob.
For more than two years, he effectively lived with another man—Albert
Johnson, the Mad Trapper—in his home and he did so with unfailingly
good humour, enthusiasm and unwavering support—all of which were
deeply appreciated.

Thanks also to editor Karla Decker for her work on this project and to
Holland Gidney, whose editing skills and encouraging words were always
so appreciated. Thank you to everyone at Heritage House—to Rodger
Touchie for his faith in the project, and especially to Vivian Sinclair, whose
patience was exceeded only by her competence.

BARBARA SMITH has written 25 bestselling
books, including *Tri* (2006), *Bathroom Book
of Canadian History* (2005), *Ghost Riders*
(2004) and *Ghost Stories of the Sea* (2003).
This is her first book for Heritage House.
Canadian social history is one of her lifelong
interests, and she has taught writing courses
in schools and for private industry. She and
her husband, Bob, live on Vancouver Island
in British Columbia.